Twice Born

by
Robert Hart
Based on the testimony of
Thomas Archer and Willow Archer

About the Author
After a career as a professional educator, Robert Hart is now an old man who lives by the sea and writes stories.

The Testimony of Thomas Archer and Willow Archer

Thomas Archer, born in 1910, was a carpenter who made fine furniture. In the summer of 1986, his granddaughter, Willow, saw a strange creature in the woods behind his cottage in Devon. Thomas later met with the creature, from whom he and his family learned of many wonders. He promised he would record what he leaned in a Journal and pass it on. Before his death, he gifted the Journal, his notebook, and letters to Willow Archer, who brought them to Robert Hart and asked him to produce this book.

Dedication
This is for: Thomas Archer's beloved wife, Naomi, their children and grandchildren, down all the generations.

Copyright

© Robert Hart 2023, © Willow Archer 2023, © Thomas Archer 1988.

The song, O Willow Waly, Copyright © George Auric and Paul Dehn

The Stolen Child, Copyright © WB Yeats

The moral right of the authors has been asserted. All rights reserved. No part of this book may be reproduced in any form or by any means without permission in writing from the publisher, except by a reviewer, or educator who may quote brief passages. This book is sold subject to the condition that it shall not, by way of trade or otherwise, be lent, resold, hired out, or otherwise circulated without the publisher's prior consent in any form of binding or cover other than that in which it is published and without a similar condition including this condition being imposed on the subsequent purchaser.

Version: 1.4

ISBN: 978-1-387-20029-0

Publisher
Published by Robert Hart 2023
Produced by Lulu.com

With grateful thanks to:
Carole Hart Fletcher – Love of my life, you are my life. Through the best of times, the worst of times, we are still, and always will be, the very best of friends.

Jim and Diana Baker – for your love and hugs, whiskey and cake, encouragement and editorial advice.

The Dartmouth SITP Sunday Club for your love, wisdom and support.

By the Same Author
Rebecca's Secrets
What happens when a boy starts asking questions?

It's New Year's day, 1956, and as the low winter sun penetrates the dark corners of Eric Street, it sets fire to a boy's curiosity.

"*Until this day I'd lived unaware. I didn't live my life — it lived me. But I did know I was different from other kids. There was something secret about me and my family. That morning I became curious. That day I started asking questions.*"

Published by Lulu.com 2009
ISBN 978-1-4092-5593-2

1

Introduction by Robert Hart

My wife and I bought a house in Kingswear, beside the Higher Ferry slipway on the banks of the River Dart. It was an unusual house with a steam train running in front of it and a wild woodland behind.

We'd lived there for a few years, when a lady knocked on our door, out of the blue. "My name is Willow Archer." She said. "My grandparents used to live here."

We invited her in for tea. Willow said she came to fulfil a promise to her grandfather. She told a remarkable story about her childhood and what she, Thomas and Naomi Archer discovered in the Hoodown Woods and how it changed their lives.

She gave me a copy of Thomas's Journal, his notebook, and letters, and she asked if I would tell their story.

Well, here it is, based on Thomas, Naomi, and Willow's testimony, the unique and fascinating story of the Twice Born.

Robert Hart
Dartmouth, Devon
January 2023

2

Introduction by Willow Archer

In 1986, when I was ten, I visited my grandfather, Thomas Archer, at his house in Devon. While I was playing in the garden, I saw a strange flying thing. It disappeared into the Hoodown Woods. Papa Tom was old and sick, but he climbed to the woods with me to find it. The thing was gone, but Papa promised he'd return to the woods and find out what it was.

What he discovered and later revealed to Grandma Naomi and me was miraculous.

He wrote down what he learned in his Journal and notebooks, and just before he died, he gave it to me. He said I had to wait ten years, then read it, and then share what we found with the World.

There were a few big surprises for me, but I can confirm that all he wrote is just as I remember. I checked with Grandma, who also confirmed everything.

I gave a copy of Papa Tom's journal, his notes, and last

letters to author, Robert Hart. I asked him to edit and present our story as he wished. We changed a few names to protect people and removed some information that might have dangerous consequences if misused. Otherwise, this book is a full and true representation of my family story. I hope you find it interesting.

Bye for now.
Willow Archer, 2023

3

Letter of Introduction by Thomas Archer

Dear Reader,

Since you are reading this, I must be dead. I made a promise. If I kept the promise, I died. If I broke the promise, I died.

This is the testimony of what I discovered in the Hoodown Woods, by the River Dart, in the county of Devon.

Today, 6th June 1986, the creatures I first met one month ago, have agreed to tell me everything I wish to know about them. I've promised I will keep a true and faithful record of what I learn in the Journal they gave me. I will report, as well as I can, what has passed so far and whatever may follow.

I promised to keep everything secret for the rest of my life and for ten years after. I will give the Journal to my granddaughter Willow who may disclose the secrets we learned down all our generations.

If you are reading this now, then my life is over and Willow has passed our story to you.

Yours Most Sincerely,
In Truth and Good Faith
Thomas Archer
6th June 1986

4

From The Journal of Thomas Archer

6th June 1986

I need to tell you how this all began.

Back in the spring, my granddaughter, Willow, was visiting me and my wife, Naomi, in our house on the banks of the River Dart.

The Dart flows from the moors beyond Totnes to Dartmouth Harbour. *Quay Cottage lies on the East bank, alongside the track of the Paignton and Dartmouth Steam Railway. It overlooks the gated level crossing by the slipway to the Higher Ferry that crosses the river to Dartmouth.

[*Quay Cottage—name changed to protect the current resident's privacy. — Willow Archer]

The rear garden winds up a cliff path into the Hoodown Woods, a dense forest of oak, sycamore and hazel that stretches a mile, along the railway track and the river to the village of Kingswear.

We bought the house, from *Joe Shepherd, who designed

and built it with his own hands. He used any materials he could rescue, scrounge or steal. He blasted stone from the cliff for the walls. He liberated oak beams from disused Navy pontoons, and he raided skips and dumps across South Devon for anything useful. The cottage was a work of art that took him eleven years to construct.

[*Joe Shepherd—*Name changed to protect his privacy.* — *Willow Archer.*]

Naomi took charge of the garden and granted me the woods as my adventure playground. I spent many hours exploring, building tree houses, clearing pathways into the forest. But recently, due to injuries and ailments, I'm no longer able to climb the steep path. So, I let the forest look after itself. That was, until Willow set me on a quest that changed all of our lives.

Willow loved the woods. Whenever she visited, she'd be first through the front door. She'd burst in, shout "Hi Grampses!" She'd give me and Naomi quick hugs and run out to the terrace.

She'd lean over the balustrade to see if the steam train was coming. If it was, she'd wave to Barrie and he'd give her a toot of the whistle that echoed across the river valley.

Then she'd skip to the garden steps, where Joe's Faerie statue stood on the wall, looking up the hill. The Faerie was one of three surprise gifts that Joe left us. He hung a note around her neck:

"Hi, Naomi and Tom. This Faerie looked after me for a long time. She will lead you up the garden path to what lies beyond. I hope you will love her and the house as much as I have." — *Joe*

Willow would stop at the statue, and ask, "Which way, Faerie?" and follow the Faerie's gaze. She'd say, "Thank you, Faerie" and skip up the steps, through the garden, to the Hoodown Woods.

But Willow never went to the woods alone.

When Roland and Gemma first brought little Willow to the house, they would lay her in the buggy on the sunny garden terrace. Once, I noticed, a single white dove flew down from the woods. She perched on a nearby branch and gently *Coo Coo Coo Coooood* a little welcome. Little Willow smiled, pointed and gurgled "Birdy" or something similar. Then it flew back unto the forest.

Over the years Birdy became Willow's pet. Now she appears whenever Willow visits and follows her around the garden. She sits on her wrist and eats seed mix from her hand. She even allows Willow to cuddle her, cupping her left hand under her white breast and stroking her wings with her right.

Since Willow developed her passion for exploring the woods, Birdy learned to wait for Willow while sitting on the Faerie's head, where she had a good view of the terrace.

Willow would say, "Come on Birdy!" And the dove would fly ahead, leading the way, into the trees.

Willow would usually be gone for over an hour, when she'd return with a gift, an acorn, or a flower, to drop at the Faerie's feet.

That's just what she did on the day our adventure began.

With Willow off exploring the Woods, we relaxed with tea and biscuits and a catch-up. Our son, Roland, told me about the startup telecoms company he'd just joined. His wife, Gemma, showed Naomi some of the fashion designs she'd drawn for her firm's winter collection. Then they planned what to cook for dinner. Roo the dog settled quickly and was dozing in the sun streaming through the garden doors. Naomi poured me a cup and added three cubes of sugar, chanting in the soft Irish lilt that I loved so much, "One for you. One for me. One for little Daisy Lee."

Willow suddenly burst in from the garden, hot and panting. Roo half-opened one eye.

"Papa, Daddy, Mummy, Come and see!"

She grabbed my sleeve and tugged hard.

"Come Papa, Grandma. Come quick. See what I've found!"

Roland and Gemma chuckled, glanced at the ceiling, smiled knowingly at each other.

Willow cupped her hands over my ear and whispered, "It's something magic, Papa, magic!"

Willow dragged me to my feet. "Any more for a trip to the woods?" I asked.

Naomi said, jokily exaggerating her County Cork accent, "Oh b'Jesus, Tom, I'd love to, but the ol' knees won't let me today."

Roo barked, "Me! Me!"

Gemma handed me Roo's lead, "Might as well take him." She said, "Double brownie points!"

So off we went, a reluctant Grandpa, an enthusiastic Willow and an over-enthusiastic black Labrador.

Willow stood in front of Joe's Faerie. She sang, "Come on, Papa!" She pirouetted and skipped nimbly up the steps. I slowly followed.

Willow is an unusual child. I've never seen her walk without skipping, or move without dancing. When she talks, she sings, each sentence a melody.

She skipped ahead up the path, then suddenly froze and pointed to the trees above and said, "Listen!"

I could hear nothing, until I realised she'd noticed the music of the rustling leaves. A little further on, she shouted, "Click!" and pointed to the sound of a click beetle in the long grass, twenty yards away. She froze and pointed when she saw a well-camouflaged green caterpillar on a green leaf among a thousand green leaves.

Gemma, jokes that Willow must have been touched by a Faerie when she was born, and she was blessed with super-sensory perception, a vivid imagination, a beautiful singing voice and a remarkable memory. "She should be a singer or an actress." Gemma once said, "She can learn her lines and everyone else's in the cast. They won't need a prompter with Willow about."

Since she was a toddler, on each visit, I'd made up a story for her. No matter how long and rambling it was, she would repeat it when she next came to see us, perhaps two months later, word for word.

She has her mother's slim form and elfin features, but no one can explain her fiery red hair, when there's not a trace of even ginger, in either family.

She chattered incessantly. "That's an oak tree, Papa. Look, you can tell by the wobble round the leaves and, look, you can see acorns and galls. The galls are hiding little wasps. That's a sycamore. The seeds are helicopters. That's a fern. That's a bracken. They look the same, but they're different. Them's brambles. They grow blackberries. That's an apple tree. That's your greenhouse because you grow green things in it."

"I grow tomatoes."

"OK, it's a redhouse."

She climbed to the edge of the garden, where Joe's second gift stood on an outcrop of granite, the marker for our boundary. It's a hideous concrete pig. Joe left a note tied to its tail which read:

"This monster was a gift from my mother. She named it Grunt. I hate it, but can't bring myself to dump it. You are welcome to keep or dispose of it as you wish." — Joe

Willow tapped the pig's rump and said, "Hi Grunt. Wait there 'til we come back."

She wriggled through a gap in the brambles into the wild woods. I followed slowly, catching glimpses of her flaming hair through the branches. Her path was one only a child could take. Not easy for a tired old man.

She danced along the deer path, parallel to the river, and turned left up a rough track through the hazel coppice. It was getting steeper. Even with Roo's help, I had to stop and catch my breath.

I heard the train on its return from Paignton. There was a toot — Naomi must have been out on the terrace — then a hiss of steam and a cloud of sooty smoke rose through the trees nearby.

"Come on, Papa!" She sang and ran into the dense woods. She skipped over fallen boughs, which I had to drag myself across painfully, joints aching and muscles burning. "I'm coming! Slow down!" I said.

"Bluebells, Papa!" She sang, "Faeries plant them."

I tripped on exposed tree roots snaking up the path. I lumbered up a scree of slate. I scrambled over a fall of boulders on hands and knees. Roo dragged me backwards through a thicket of hazel, then a wall of brambles.

"Come on, Papa."

I caught up with Willow in a grassy clearing. I knew this place. I'd been here long before, when I used to explore deep in the woods. It was rare to find a sunny clearing in this dense forest. It had a special calmness about it.

From here we could see The Britannia Royal Naval College, glinting in the sun, high above the West bank of the River.

Willow said, "That's where Prince Phillip learned how to be a sailor. That's where he met the Queen, and they got married and lived happily ever after."

The far end of the clearing, was cut across by a hanging valley, which ran East to West to create a deep gorge. It was about thirty feet wide and just as deep, opening up as it fell towards the river.

From the forest above, a rocky stream ran through the clearing, curled away from us, to the south and cascaded into the gorge. Willow stood near the waterfall, before a huge tree.

"Papa. It's a Faerie Tree!" She spread her arms to encompass the blasted oak behind her.

Its trunk leaned at ten degrees towards the edge of the gorge, so, one third of the canopy spread over the void. Twenty feet up, a main bough had been struck by lightning and partly torn from the trunk. Willow's white dove perched on the lightning wound. The bough stretched almost horizontally over the clearing, the furthest branches just touching the grass.

Lightning had severed another two boughs which had fallen in front of the trunk one on the other like a giant's fat fingers, crossed for luck. They were covered by a curtain of ivy, and a coat of lichen, and moss.

Willow pointed to the dark opening between the curve of the giant's fingers.

"It was there, Papa, The flying thing. It was a Faerie! I saw it right there. It flew past me." She waved her arm over her shoulder.

"Willow," I said, still trying to catch my breath, "this is the certainly perfect place for Faeries and today is the perfect day. It's the twentieth of March, the astrological first day of spring. A wonderful day to meet a Faerie."

"But it's gone now." She said, looking back with a frown and a pout.

I shuffled towards her. "What did it look like?"

"It was a brown, blurry thing. I couldn't really see much, but when it vanished, I thought of a skinny little person with dragonfly wings."

"You thought?"

"Well, I saw it in my head."

"OK. Let's see if it comes back."

We sat on the grass in front of the tree. A bumble bee buzzed by, a dragonfly, a red admiral. A hive bee rested on my knee. A gang of sparrows argued in a nearby bush. A buzzard circled above.

No Faeries.

"Perhaps we frightened it away." I said.

"Well, you were puffing like the steam train, Papa."

"Cheeky girl! You'll be puffing at my age. I'm seventy-six, you know, and I'm nearly falling to bits!"

"I know, Papa, but you reached the top of the cliff this time. You can do it again. You must come back and find the flying Faerie thing. I can't. I'm going home tomorrow."

"I will, Willow. I'll come back." I said.

"Will you come back every day, Papa? To our Faerie Tree, in our Faerie Glen? Every single day until you find the Faerie? Will you? Will you promise?"

I glanced back at the challenging path we'd taken. I took a deep breath, rubbed my knees and, knowing I would regret it, I said, "I promise."

"And will you 'phone me when you see it?"

"Of course I will."

"Thank you, Papa."

The Naval College clock chimed.

"Eight bells, Afternoon Watch, Papa. Time for lunch. I'll go help Grandma."

"I'll be right behind you." I said, knowing that I wouldn't.

Willow said, "Don't forget a gift for Joe's Faerie!" She floated off down the path. Roo bounded after her.

I followed slowly, slipping down the scree on my arse, stumbling over the rockfall, cursing my painful hips and knees. It took me about fifteen minutes to reach the terrace.

I dropped an acorn beside the one Willow had placed at the Faerie's feet. Willow was helping Naomi cut some roses. They'd collected a dozen stems in a basket.

"You were slow, Papa." Willow said, "We've done all this gardening."

"She loves to help her Grandma." Naomi said, with a proud smile. "These are for Gemma to take home."

"Shall I put some in a vase for you, Grandma?" Willow said.

Naomi replied, "No, thank you, darling." She glanced at me. "I don't like to watch beautiful things die."

As Willow and our kids drove away, she waved furiously with the broadest of grins. She shouted, "Bye, Papa! Keep looking!"

I shouted after, "I will. Bye for now."

Before Willow came running in from the woods that day, I hadn't given much thought to Faeries. I learned a poem at school, *The Stolen Child* by W.B. Yates. Here's the part I remember, the last verse:

Come away! O, human child!
To the woods and waters wild.
With a Faerie hand-in-hand,
For the world's more full of weeping than
You can understand.

Naomi, though, often talked about Faeries. It was a big thing in her Irish family. She said her mother, Eleanor, was very superstitious and was always going on about what you should and shouldn't do, when Faeries were around.

At bedtime, you had to stoke the fire, leave a drop of beer in your glass and put out a saucer of milk and a biscuit, to make the Wee Folk feel welcome when they came at night. If you were sure a Faerie was in the house, you had to wear something inside out. In the morning, the first one down should whistle on the stairs to warn the Faeries, and give them time to leave or hide.

Eleanor had many such beliefs, which she drummed into Naomi and her brother, William. In fact, he grew so fed up with his mother's obsessions that he wrote a book in which he mercilessly exposed people who thought they'd seen Faeries, ghosts or spirits, and lambasted them as complete fools.

Naomi always claimed she didn't really believe any of her mother's Faerie nonsense, but I'm not so sure. I've noticed she always puts another log on the fire at bedtime and some nights I've noticed she wears her pyjamas inside out.

Naomi told me once, after a few glasses of ginger wine, that Eleanor believed Faeries stole human children. Well, to me elves, goblins, and Faeries are all the stuff of dreams and childish nonsense, but I suspect Naomi is truly wary of Faerie Folk, and I've decided not to share Willow's whispers of magical creatures for now. Instead, I told Naomi I enjoyed climbing to the woods, and I'd decided to go again the next day. She shrugged and said, "Oh well, you do what you like, Tom, s'long as you're not under my feet."

While I don't believe in Faeries, I do believe in children

and the special sensitivities some have. To Willow, her flying fuzzy thing is something real in her mind, and that's good enough for me. I promised I'd look for her Faerie every day. A promise is a promise.

To help me enter into the spirit of this Faerie hunt. I tried to imagine, if Faeries existed, what they might think about humans. For example, Faeries might like young children, but not be keen on old folk. Maybe they wouldn't like the smell of old humans, so I started out early, fresh from the shower at eight bells on the Forenoon Watch.

The first climb by myself was a challenge without Willow and Roo to distract me from the effort. I had to take it very slowly and rest often. On the way I slipped, tripped and fell too many times to enjoy the walk. I feared I might have to break my promise. This could be my first and only effort.

When I finally arrived in the clearing, I was aching all over, panting and disgustingly sweaty.

I sat on a moss-covered log, in front of Willow's Faerie Tree. It was saturated with the night dew. I jumped up and searched for a better spot. There wasn't one, so I spread my anorak over the log and settled in for my vigil. I slowed my breath and kept still.

Beams of morning sunlight slanted through the branches of the oak, painting dappled shadows across the grassy bank and highlighting the bluebells. The higher branches twisted and crossed each other like strangely elbowed human arms holding up the sunlit canopy. I didn't see Willow's dove. She never showed up unless Willow was around.

The stream sparkled as it tumbled down the hill and disappeared between the tree-giant's fingers into the shadows beyond.

I saw no unusual flying things.

I continued with this painful pilgrimage for a week. I tried to make each trip a little easier. I took a fold-up fisherman's chair to place before the tree and a plastic bin liner to keep it dry overnight. I tied rope between some of the tree trunks to pull myself over the steeper parts. I juggled larger rocks into rough steps and, when I felt strong enough, I dragged a plank of wood on a rope and made a bridge across the scree.

It was hard, but I was doing it for Willow, so that next time she visited, I could honestly say I'd kept my promise and watched out for her Faerie thing every single day.

On the seventh day, Naomi, decided my morning walk to the woods was settling into a habit. She said it was good for my health and her sanity. So, each day she made a flask of coffee and stuffed it into a rucksack with some biscuits.

On the tenth day, I had a surprise. I'd been sitting quietly for nearly an hour. I reached for my coffee, when something streaked from the shadows between the fallen boughs and buzzed past my face. It was brownish and bigger than a dragonfly. I couldn't quite make it out, but it was like nothing I'd ever seen before.

Over the following week I saw the brown blurry thing every other day and then every day and then several times each day.

I had no idea what it was. I rang Willow and told her I'd seen a large insect thing fly out of the tree. She was so excited. She said I must keep going back.

A few days later, I'd dozed off in the warm sunshine and as I woke, my eyes bleary, I saw a twitch among the leaves. I peered towards the movement, but saw nothing but leaves. Then I caught the twitch again. I kept my eyes half-closed, peering through my lashes.

It was like looking at one of those illusion drawings in a psychology book, where you see a rabbit with big floppy ears, and then it suddenly turns into a lady with a feathery hat. After that, you only see the lady and the rabbit's gone forever. As I stared at the leaves, the shades of green and brown merged into something.

It looked vaguely like a tiny person, with body, arms, legs, and a head with hair that appeared to be on fire!

I cried out, "Oh!" It disappeared instantly, as if it'd been switched off. I stayed another hour, but it didn't return. *Just a trick of the light*, I thought.

The next day, I didn't see it. I peered into the green and saw only green. But I was beginning to enjoy the walk, so I returned the next day and the next.

On Sunday morning. I'd been sitting for twenty minutes when I saw a fast-moving blur. It stopped and hovered over the fallen boughs. I kept my mouth shut tight and didn't move. This must've been the right thing to do because it came back every day after that, always twenty minutes after I arrived. Or perhaps it was there all along but only showed itself after I'd had twenty minutes of quiet meditation, bathing in the beauty of the forest and becoming attuned to the shifting patterns of light.

I realised I had to build trust if this creature was to return. For days, I sat quietly and watched. As it hovered over the log, I studied its form, like an artist who sketches a picture in his mind before he puts brush to canvas.

Each time I saw it, the form became a little clearer. I couldn't think of it as '*it*' any more, since it was definitely human-like in form, and it looked vaguely female. She was about six inches tall. The body was covered in a translucent sheen, like lace or gossamer. Her arms and legs were longer and more slender in proportion than a human. Her face was fine featured, with a long slim nose and prominent cheek bones. Her eyes were large and deeply dark. Her hair was red, yellow, and white and the colours seemed to move, dancing like flames.

As she hovered, she looked around, her eyes resting on me for a moment then flitting away.

I knew it couldn't possibly be true, but this thing really did look like some kind of Faerie creature.

The next day, she gazed at me more directly. She nodded slightly. As if to acknowledge, she'd seen me. She watched me with an expression that wavered between curious and wary.

I gazed back day after day with what, I thought, was an encouraging smile. One day, she gave me a shy smile back. I tried not to show it, but I was thrilled this amazing creature had acknowledged me.

She came to trust me enough to come closer, sometimes hovering within a foot of my face. Occasionally she landed on a twig from an overhanging branch. I would remain calm and still, not daring to talk or move.

Then one morning, after quietly watching each other, she came to rest on the arm of my fisherman's chair, on the edge of the cup-holder.

She closed her wings and turned her back to me, as if to show she felt safe. After that, she stayed a little longer each time until we sat together for about ten minutes every day, before she flew off to do whatever these creatures do.

I decided it was time to tell Naomi I'd seen Willow's

Faerie-insect-thing. She laughed, "Tom, you're as fanciful as that wee child. I think you never grew up, and you never want to."

"You could be right." I said, "You usually are."

"Usually?" She raised her eyebrows.

5

When Willow's Faerie thing hovered before me this morning, she made her first communication – in mime. She placed her hands together palms-up in the shape of a bowl and lifted the bowl to her lips and raised her head, as if drinking. She pointed to the stream flowing near the fallen oak boughs. She flew there and hovered over a small pool, held back by a rock, before the stream cascaded over the cliff into the ravine.

I followed her and she repeated the drinking gesture. I knelt and scooped water from the pool into my hands and drank.

I've never tasted anything so fresh and pure. It fizzed on my tongue and flowed down my throat like an ocean wave. It was cold and hot at the same time, like an aged Irish malt whiskey.

It cooled and burned its way to my stomach and coursed

through my body until it rose like a tsunami in my head and boosted all my senses.

The world began to spin. I saw new colours – ultra-blue and infra-red. The shadows beneath the trees became lighter, and to my great wonder, I saw a host of Faerie things flitting between the branches. Their wings were iridescent, with jewelled highlights of impossible colours, deep green, bright turquoise. They flew to and fro, meeting, touching, parting, going about their lives. Some glanced briefly towards me, a few smiled and flew on their way.

When I looked back at my Faerie insect friend, my eyes popped wide. Her wispy hair flowed the whole length of her body and beyond, flowing around her as if blown in a gentle breeze. It was flaming red, orange, yellow, and white. Her eyes were deep blue and her silvery wings were sprinkled with sapphire stars.

I was a grinning idiot, transfixed by the spectacle before me. I was flabbergasted to think that this fabulous creature had accepted me, and allowed me to see how beautiful she was.

I know I'm old and sick and people think I'm a bit over imaginative. This could all be some kind of delirium episode, but, against a lifetime of cynicism, I was starting to believe this was a real Faerie.

My Faerie friend hovered before me. She looked into my

eyes. She placed her palms together as if in prayer and bowed. She spread her arms to encompass the Faerie world I could now see around her. Then she disappeared into the woody gloom.

As I descended the path home, my head was spinning. *This can't be true. But it's happening. They're really Faeries. They can't be. I'm hallucinating. No, it's real.*

My feet floated across the screes. I danced a hop-scotch over the rock-fall and skipped down the garden steps, avoiding creatures I'd not noticed before. A water rat ran from the cliff, crossed the step and dived towards the river. A grass snake quivered and sloped away under a bush.

I sat for a while on the terrace watching the river. I saw grey mullet grazing in the shallows under a small cloud of midges.

When my excitement had settled, I greeted Naomi as calmly as I could.

"I saw them, Nay, Willow's Faeries. I saw lots of them."

She looked to the sky, smiled indulgently and said, "That's nice, Tom. Want to see my boat? I've finished it at last."

She led me to the attic room. Her studio was a tiny space in a corner behind a Japanese paper screen.

"Ta dah!" She said, pulling a dust-sheet from her easel.

I've always loved Naomi's paintings. She focussed on ordinary things you see every day but don't see at all. She brought out the colours and shapes, so they seemed to flip from being objects to abstracts. But now I saw something very different.

"I call it The Rotting Hulk." She said.

It was the prowl of a fishing boat that I recognised. We'd seen it, washed up on the beach and left to rot near Fishnish on the West coast of the Isle of Mull. It had been painted in successive layers of blue, which had flaked off to reveal earlier layers of green and orange. The colours were amazing, and each plank carried the imprint of its past, a dent, a crack, a channel worn by a line. But there was more.

In my mind, I saw the fishermen who worked on her. I felt this craft was the centre of their life. I sensed their years of dedication to keep the ship in good condition. It was their livelihood. I saw them struggling against the elements – the howling wind, the cutting rain, the wild ocean clutching at their feet. I felt their elation when they hauled in a great catch, saw the joyful reception from their families when they landed. I also felt how an empty net meant heartache and hunger for their children. Naomi had recorded their whole lives with each stroke of her brush.

"It's... magical, Nay," I said, "Beautiful."

Without thinking, I held out my arms to give her a hug, but she stepped back a little, and we settled for appreciative smiles.

That afternoon, I was due to meet a few of my mates in the park. I said, "I'm going over the river, Nay. Do you want to come with me to see the old boys, or join me later for a coffee at Bayards?"

Naomi said, "You go ahead Tom, I'll finish up here and I'll see you on the other side."

We did meet later at the Bayard's Inn and took coffee together. While we sat in the busy cafe, I said, "I do love your work, Nay. Your art is very special."

She said, "Thank you."

I said, "And I do love you, no matter what we have been through."

"I know." She said.

She squeezed my hand and there was a hint of tearfulness in her eyes.

I know Naomi loves me and cares for me, as I do for her, but a veil of sadness has come between us and will not go away. It's as if tiny spiders, hide in the dark corners of our memories and over the years, they have spun little cobwebs to obscure our joy and trust in each other.

In the evening, I called Willow and told her what had happened at the Glen. After she stopped laughing and screaming into the phone, she said, "Papa, you've been given a Faerie gift. A real Faerie let you see her. You must always return a Faerie's gift."

"Mmm. I'm not very good at gifts."

What can you give a Faerie? What did I have that would be of any use or have any meaning to such an exotic creature? I thought long and hard and slept on the idea. By morning, I had my answer.

I made my way back to the Glen and when my Faerie friend hovered before me, in all her glorious colours, I copied her prayer-hands gesture.

I felt very self-conscious as I said aloud, "I thank you for allowing me to see you and your people. I would like to learn about you. I would like to understand what I can do for you."

I took, from my pocket, a bay leaf I'd folded to make a tiny envelope. I placed it on the arm of the chair.

I said, "You have given me the precious gift of pure spring water that opened my eyes to your world. I would like to offer a gift in return, but I have nothing so magical for you. Please accept this small token."

She flew down, perched on the arm of the chair, and carefully unfolded the leaf, while I watched nervously. When she saw what was inside she turned, looked at me and smiled. She took up the postage-stamp-sized image of Willow that I'd cut from a family group photo.

I said, "This is Willow, my granddaughter. You met her. I think you sent her to me, and I think she sent me to you. This is a little token of Willow, I'm sure she would like you to keep."

The Faerie smiled broadly and nodded her thanks.

I was happy with my silent relationship with my flame-haired Faerie friend and wished for nothing more. On my next visit, she came to my chair holding something green in her long-fingered hands. She laid it on the arm of the chair, flew back and hovered before me.

It was a Pennywort leaf, a fleshy green circle an inch across. On the leaf, a golden blob of what looked like honey. I carefully reached for it and sniffed. It smelled like honey, but there was a heady over-scent I didn't recognise. I looked at her and she nodded. I scooped the honey on to my finger and licked.

At first, I heard a quiet buzzing, like the hum of a bee hive. That faded, and my ears became more sensitive. I felt like a deaf person using a hearing aid for the first time. But I didn't just hear the surrounding sounds, I felt them. They resonated throughout my body.

She pointed both forefingers at me. She clenched her fists over her ears and slowly opened her fingers, like flowers opening. Fingers wide, she spread her hands taking in the sky, the tree canopy, the grassy bank and the undergrowth.

I thought she was inviting me to open my ears and listen

to everything.

I heard, and then I felt, the usual sounds of the woods – a sharply amplified mix of leaves sighing in the breeze, insects buzzing, birds chirping, water trickling.

After a few seconds, I made out a distant wood pigeon *coo-cooing* and a robin chirping nearby. A gang of sparrows chattered in a bush fifty yards away. A buzzard mewled overhead. Another pigeon *coo-cooed* to the first. Two more Robins, deep in the woods, took turns to respond. A pair of herring gulls kraaked angrily and dive-bombed the buzzard until it flew sulkily away. Another gang of gulls, out of sight, over the river, cried in a feeding frenzy as they dived into a shoal of mackerel. A pair of shelducks cried 'peep peep' and darted downriver, in close formation, straight and low and out to sea.

I heard again the hum of hive bees in the trees above, then a deep drone of a bumblebee, the head-drilling whine of a mosquito, the click of a beetle deep in the woods.

The Faerie repeated the open-your-ears gesture.

I listened more intently. Over the tinkling of the stream I heard another lighter tinkling from the dark between the fallen boughs. Beneath this, a light humming and rasping. These new sounds, that must have been there all the time, gradually resolved into whispers and giggles – a few at first, that quickly grew into a multitude.

Soon I could distinguish hundreds of voices, speaking in what sounded like all the languages of the world at the same time. I closed my eyes and concentrated, and I was amazed to pick out a few words in Gaelic, Spanish, Russian, French, Hebrew, and English.

I focussed my attention on the English. A few recognisable words: 'tree', 'stream', 'flower'. The words resolved into phrases. But I couldn't make sense of it. Gradually it settled into English with a strong Irish accent and more words became clear.

The multitude of voices coalesced into a chorus speaking in unison and then into the voice of a single human child, uncannily like the voice of Willow.

"You have the Hearing, Human. Tomorrow, we will speak."

I was thrilled! When I arrived home I couldn't wait to call Willow.

"Willow, the Faeries gave me some honey. Now I can hear them talking. In fact, I can hear plenty of things I couldn't hear before – acorns falling, seeds popping, flowers opening, squirrels chewing acorns a hundred yards away. I can even hear rumbles when the clouds bump into each other."

"That's wonderful, Papa!"

"They said they'll speak with me, Willow!"

"Oh Papa! You'll be able to find out all about them, ask lots of questions. What present shall we give them back?"

"I don't know. What can we give them?"

"Well… they gave you their voices. We must give them our voices."

"How do we do that?"

"I could sing for them, Papa. I know a song they will like. Mummy used to sing it, to send me to sleep. I'll record it and send you a cassette."

The next few days, I couldn't go to the woods. I had bad stomach ache and digestive system problems I won't go into.

On my next trip I took my portable cassette player, a present from Roland and Gemma, and the tape that arrived from Willow.

When the Faerie appeared, I said, "I am sorry I couldn't see you. I have been ill. But I am well now, and I have a little something to thank you for giving me the sound of your voices. It's the voice of my granddaughter with a song for you. I hope you like it."

I pressed play on the Walkman and Willow's voice wafted into the Glen.

'We lay my love and I beneath the weeping willow.
But now alone I lie and weep beside the tree.
Singing 'Oh willow waly'

*By the tree that weeps with me.
Singing 'Oh willow waly'
'Til my lover return to me.
We lay my love and I beneath the weeping willow.
A broken heart have I. Oh willow I die, oh willow I die."*

A cloud of Faeries flew from the trees and hovered around us, listening. Then they sang the song back in the most exquisite harmonies, and their voices filled the forest.

"This be song of mother." The Faerie said.

I was delighted to hear her gentle voice and shocked at what she knew. I hadn't told her it was Gemma's favourite lullaby.

Naomi was on the terrace, when I returned, setting out a salad lunch.

"I thought you'd like a pint of Guinness for a treat." She said, "What've you been up to in the woods?"

"I played them this tape from Willow." I said and pressed the button on the Walkman.

"That's so pretty, Tom. She sings like an angel. I know that song."

Naomi had played the fiddle since she was a young child. She told me she had never had lessons. It just came to her. She could play any song. She only had to hear it once and she could play it perfectly, as if she'd been playing it for years, with her fluid bowing and subtle ornamentation, rolls, trebles, and cuts. In fact, you could tell her the title of a song she'd never heard before and she'd still play it perfectly. I used to ask her, "Where did you hear that one, Nay?" She'd say, "Oh somewhere, sometime. I dunno."

"Will you play it for me, Nay?"

She hesitated, then smiled and slipped into the house. She returned with her fiddle. She played *Oh Willow Waly*, a dreamy modal air.

I've always loved her playing. It was more than music that came from her fiddle. When I was sick or down, she would play for me and I'd feel a little better straight away. There was never a person in any room where Naomi played who would not feel an injection of joy and well-being coming from her music.

But today it was different. I was inside the music and the music was inside me. I could feel each note vibrate through my whole body and resonate in my chest and my skull. I had an unusually clear vision of the children, Roland and Gemma, lying in each other's arms beneath a Willow tree. The chorus of Faeries scattered in the branches above sang, "We lay my love and I beneath the weeping willow. Oh, Willow I die, oh willow I die."

6

I climbed to our Faerie Glen, with excitement bubbling in my chest. I could see them. I could hear them. Now I might learn from them.

My Faerie came from under the fallen boughs, hovered before me, and spoke in faltering English.

"Human," She said, "Now you have the Seeing, the Hearing. We speak. First, you promise. Three times."

I was puzzled, but I said, "Of course, I will promise whatever you want."

"Promise one. Keep true record of our speaking. What you learn, you write with own hand."

"I would love to do that."

"You keep us secret. Keep Faeries safe your Earth time."

"But I've already told my wife, Naomi, I've seen you and Willow knows."

"Willow is friend. Wife is wise. She say not."

I'd realised that no one would believe me if I mentioned Faeries at the bottom of my garden and, if anyone did, I didn't want a queue of tourists at the cottage coming to take snaps of the Hoodown Faerie Glen. I'd already decided to keep their secret.

I said, "I promise that."

"Human, promise two. When Earth time done. You pass your learning down all your generations."

I said, "I promise that"

"We thank Human for promises." She said, "Soon we show our ways."

"And, the third promise?" I asked.

"Later." She flew into the dark.

I sat awhile thinking how strange life had become. *I'm talking to a Faerie! Perhaps not. Maybe it's an hallucination brought on by my cancer? Or my medicines?*

I do take a handful of pills each day. One for blood pressure to protect the heart from strain, a blood thinner to keep strokes away, cholesterol scrubbers to keep my arteries clean and three more to counter the side effects of those three.

Back at the cottage, I checked the Adverse Reactions section on the Patient Information leaflet for each pill. They listed plenty of nasty side effects, but none caused hallucinations.

At last the day has come. I've promised to keep the Faeries safe, to make a record of our conversations and keep them secret while I live, and then pass the Faeries' wisdom down my generations. The Faeries promised to teach me their ways. Now it begins.

I climbed to my fisherman's chair with a flask of coffee and waited for my Faerie friend.

She appeared, hovering before me.

I said aloud, "Thank you for agreeing to speak with me. I don't know how we should conduct this conversation."

She said, "Ask questions, Human. We answer."

"*We* answer?" I asked.

"I speak for all Faerie. I am one. I am all. All in one voice. What you say me, you say all."

"So," I said, "Where should we start?"

There was no answer.

"Well, er… I am called Thomas."

"You name Human."

"Yes, my people are called Human, but my personal name is Thomas."

"Yes."

I waited for a reciprocal response. It didn't come.

"Er… and will you tell me your name?"

"You can not speak it."

"Please, let me try."

"My name is…"

I heard a trilling whistle, followed by clicks, rather like the robin's song but more complex. Written down, it might look like: *Pweez-ummp-ststipippa-zerxcchix*.

"I see what you mean. Can you say it in English."

"It not be in English. I know what Thomas want. You call me… Tinkerbell."

I couldn't help chuckling. *Do Faeries have a sense of humour?* I thought. "So you know about our fairy stories?"

"We teach you. We know you long time. We live by you thousands years. You want new Faerie name? Call me… Dolly Toadwhiskey!"

I laughed.

"Not good? Call me… Fiona Rumpletwhistle, Amnesia Shimmerfoot, Marshmallow Twinkledandy, Wildfire Hollyprickle." She sang.

I scratched my head.

"Shiny Aspenfrog, Lunabell Lillyflower, Daisy Butterslip, Turniphead Watermouse, Moonbeam Winterbramble?"

"Er… they're like storybook Faerie names." I said.

"That what Thomas Human like?" She said.

"How about… Sapphire, for the colour of your eyes?" I suggested.

"That good." She said, "We agree. The Naming. You Thomas we Sapphire."

She smiled, clapped her hands, flew a little figure-of-eight dance and disappeared into the tree.

I took that as my cue to leave.

I asked, Sapphire, "Will you please tell me why your stream water tastes so wonderful?"

She said, "Water come deep under ground. From rain. It fall thousands years. Air was pure. It washed clean by stone from Earth young. Where is your water come, Thomas?"

"The Tap." I said, and seeing the questioning tilt of her head, I tried again, "The rain?"

She looked to the sky, I followed her gaze. I saw the criss-cross of jet trails slowly spreading and joining into a thin veil of chemical mist.

Then something strange happened. I saw the sky as if through her eyes.

I saw raindrops condense around tiny chemical particles. The rain fell on the fields, as farmers spread fertilizer and pesticide. I saw the rain seep across the land, collecting effluent from the cattle and sheep. I saw the beasts' blood swimming with synthetic hormones.

The rain flowed into streams and rivers, lakes and reservoirs and into treatment facilities. It joined with the street and sewage water, the human urine contaminated with pharmaceutical residues and poisons from their food. Then I saw Naomi run the kitchen tap and offer me a glass of fresh water.

I'd had my first Faerie lesson. "I understand," I said, "We should all drink water as pure as your stream, but we don't have a spring near the house."

"Water from the east. From this day, drink only pure." She said, and flew back into the tree.

When I arrived home, I looked behind the house. To the east was a thirty feet high cliff wall, completely covered by a thick curtain of Ivy, about six inches deep. I scanned the cliff face, but there wasn't a drip of water. Then, from a spot five feet up, a family of sparrows burst from cover and flew off, twittering loudly, leaving a small opening behind him.

I looked closely into the gap in the vine and saw a grey circle of exposed scree beneath. In the centre of the circle was a single pennywort leaf. I lifted the leaf and a trickle of water oozed beneath it, between the flakes of shale. I brushed the shale away and the trickle became stronger. In a while it was running like a slow tap.

From the house I brought a clean galvanized steel bucket, which I wedged under the flow. I scooped up a handful of water. It tasted pure and clean, like the Faeries' water.

Later I returned to find the bucket was full and excess water was lightly spilling over the rim and soaking back into the shale. I made a lean-to wooden canopy over the bucket to prevent contamination from the rain. Thanks to the Faeries, and their friends the sparrows, we now had our own spring of pure clean water from long ago and deep under the cliff.

Naomi was delighted that we'd found our own fresh water. Each morning, I filled two galvanized buckets – enough for drinking, making tea and cooking. After that, we used the tap water only for bathing and washing clothes.

When we met today, Sapphire said, "Now I question, Thomas."

"Yes, please ask me anything." I said.

"You be honest?"

"Of course."

"When you visit, Thomas, you fall in chair. You breathe heavy. You weary?"

"Well, yes, I do get exhausted from the climb."

"Why, Thomas? Your grandchild walk easy?"

"Well, you see, she's ten years old, and I'm seventy seven."

"I seventeen thousand, six hundred, twenty three years." Sapphire said, "In this dimension."

"That's amazing!" I said, "We don't have long lives like that. We only have eighty years, maybe a hundred if we're very lucky."

"We know human life short this time. There be reasons. I tell later. But, Thomas, being old is not a disease. It is honour. You no need be sick or tired."

"I've had several heart attacks over the past years, so my breathing isn't great, and I live with cancer. My doctors give me pills, but they make my joints ache and my muscles weak."

"When here, you also look sad."

"Well, I guess that's also about getting old and not being able to do what I could as a young man. I think the pills make me low sometimes. And, if I'm being really honest, I have regrets in my life. Sometimes I worry about the dark things that go on in the world. I drink too much whisky some nights to forget. But being here and seeing you cheers me up no end."

"We think there is more." She said.

Sapphire had been talking in English with me for only a short time. She was becoming slowly more fluent, but today I saw her tap into an amazing source of learning. She hovered silently for a few minutes, looking skyward, her eyes darting left and right, as if listening. She closed her eyes, breathed deeply and disappeared. A minute later, she reappeared and smiled.

"Where did you go?" I asked.

When she spoke again. Her fluency had shifted into top

gear. It was no longer like English as a second language or, for Faerie folk, a twentieth language.

"Thomas. I went to learn. As you will have noticed, I have not been fluent in your language. That is because we are not accustomed to speaking aloud in modern English. When we speak out-loud between ourselves, it is mostly in Gaelic mixed with a little Farsi, a smatter of Hindi, fragments of Hebrew, Aramaic, Tamil, Sanskrit, and other ancient languages we've picked up over the millennia. We rarely communicate in spoken words with humans."

"It only took a minute of your Earth time, Thomas, but I tapped into the One Mind for two years, and listened to every conversation we had with human friends over that time. Now I can use the full subtlety of your current English. It will be better for us."

I realised I was staring with my mouth wide open.

"Two years in… one minute?" I said.

"Yes. I will tell you about it another time." She said.

"Now, Thomas, I have noticed your mind is poisoned. Like many humans, you see your world through a veil of woe. Everything you perceive is distorted, shaded in dark meaning. Your mind is tainted with sadness, loss, regret, fear, suspicion, shame, and anger. These thoughts and feelings are toxic in excess. They inhibit your experience of joy and delight, and they obscure the beauty in your life. They steal your energy and infuse your body with pain."

My mouth was wide open again. I couldn't believe it was the same person, I mean, Faerie, speaking. How could she learn so much so fast?

"Your skin and hair are soaked in poison." She said, "It is in your perspiration. It is in the shoes and garments you wear, the things you touch. It is in your breath. You spread it to the people and creatures you meet."

"Is there any hope for me?" I asked.

"As long as you have curiosity and playfulness, there is hope. Thomas, you have promised to keep our secrets. Will you accept our protection in return?"

"What do you mean?"

"We will help you be well."

"Can't do any harm", I thought. "I guess so." I said.

"When you return, will you please bring your medicines?"

"I will."

"We will talk again when the sun rises." She said, and disappeared into the darkness under the trees.

The next day I puffed up the cliff path and slumped in the chair to catch my breath.

Sapphire appeared and hovered before me. She said, "Thomas, please stand."

She flew in circles, spiralling slowly around me, starting at my feet, finishing above my head.

"May I ask, what you're doing?" I said.

"I have been reading your body, so we can diagnose your health needs."

"And.. what do you find?"

"Excuse me for a moment." She said. "I just need to check a few things."

Sapphire hovered before me. She looked to the sky, her eyes searching left and right. She closed her eyes and breathed deeply. She vanished and returned a minute later.

"Have you been…?" I asked.

"Yes, I just visited the One Mind for…"

"… Two years?" I asked.

"Yes Thomas."

"Do you know what might be wrong with me?"

"Yes Thomas. We know how to help you."

"Will you tell me what's wrong?"

"You do not need to know, in order for our remedies to help." Sapphire said.

"I understand, but I would like to know anyway." I said.

"Thomas, I do not advise it." Sapphire said, "You see, diagnosis can be a curse. It has been for many years, since your adoption of scientific medicine."

"How can that be?" I asked.

"It works like this: Your doctor carries out some tests

and tells you he believes you might have an affliction in a certain organ, perhaps your heart. You have been taught since you were a child to trust and believe your doctor."

"When your family, friends and neighbours ask 'How are you today, Tom?' you tell them what your doctor said, and now they all believe you are sick. They say 'Oh, that's terrible, Tom, we hope your heart will recover.' Your communal belief in the terrible affliction manifests in your mind as a deep fear. The fear sends stress directly to your heart. The heart begins to show symptoms of stress. It deteriorates."

"The next time you see your doctor, he finds his expectations have been met. He says, 'Your heart is getting worse Tom. There are distinct symptoms of stress.' His diagnosis is confirmed. Your fear is compounded and more stress attacks your heart. You spiral down to illness."

"Still," I said, "I'd rather know what I'm dealing with."

"Thomas, I really do not advise it. If I tell you, then the shock of diagnosis might work against the remedies."

"Please, Sapphire," I said, "tell me anyway."

Sapphire took a deep breath, then, talking rapidly she said, "You have fungus in your toenails and on the soles of your feet. The lateral ligament in your left knee and the right groin tendon have been torn. The injuries were repaired by your doctors long ago, but they still give you pain and inhibit movement. Your prostate is swollen, which affects your bladder control and makes you worry about being incontinent. It may have the beginnings of cancer."

I was transfixed with the depth of her knowledge and her command of medical language. "How do you know all this?"

"Thomas, Faerie life has been long, tens of thousands of years. We have learned much from watching your intellectual and social growth down all the millennia. We have learned from observing and talking with your scientists, philosophers, and healers. Each of us has access to the knowledge and experience of all the Faeries who ever lived. My visit to the One Mind brought me up to date."

She continued: "A cancerous tumour is growing in your colon. You have a hiatus hernia, which gives you chronic indigestion. Your spine has been subject to spondylitis and disc damage. You have a trapped nerve, which causes chronic sciatica and pain in the left leg. You had tuberculosis in late childhood, which was cleared, but has reduced your lung capacity and left your breathing restricted. Impurities in your blood have caused three heart attacks, two strokes and a transient ischaemic attack, which your doctor falsely diagnosed as migraine."

I was amazed that she could tell so much, but also appalled at what had become of my body. Still she continued.

"Both of your shoulders are experiencing muscular degeneration. Your muscle and joint limitations reduce your confidence. They cause you to move defensively and prevent you from stretching and balancing naturally."

"And they ache and keep me awake at night." I said.

"Toxins in your drugs, attack your skin and lead to excessive bruising and randomly occurring lesions. Your teeth are mostly intact, but brittle and liable to break under stress."

"I broke a tooth eating pork crackling. I had to pay the dentist fifty pounds to fix it." I said.

"You had, what your doctors called, a lazy left eye in childhood that was not properly treated, leaving the eye unable to clearly focus. Pollen and spores, give you occasional hay fever, streaming eyes, snuffles, and coughs. Your hearing has been dulled."

"Your brain has been traumatised by life shocks, which you erased from your accessible memory. Medicaments have also poisoned your brain, so you suffer from melancholy, which you try to smother with addictive behaviours."

My jaw dropped. My eyes widened. I made a lame joke, "I must prepare my funeral music."

"Apart from that, you are quite healthy for a human of your age and there is much we can do to help."

"Well, that's encouraging." I said, trying to sound positive.

"Now, please show me your pills." Sapphire said.

I held out my plastic pill organiser, which had the pills

sorted in chambers by day of week.

"Place the pills for today in your right hand."

I held out my hand, palm up. She flew circles around my hand, stopped and hovered before me.

"The big pink pills help clean your blood of fatty deposits, but they also weaken your muscles and make your joints ache. The green and yellow pill is designed to improve your mood, but it makes you more sad. It causes you to be detached from others and lowers your confidence."

"Thomas, your body is swimming in harmful chemicals, but, we can help you."

"I am very grateful for your help." I said.

Sapphire said. "Have you ever been harmed by touching, eating or drinking anything natural?"

"Like allergies, you mean?"

"Yes."

"Well, I've had a few hospital trips for severe anaphylactic shock, from eating shellfish, once from a snake bite and once from a toad. In fact, the toad nearly killed me."

She was playing close attention.

"What happened with the toad?"

"Well, Naomi was in the garden one night when she saw a toad on the terrace. She's afraid of creepy things. She yelled for me to come take the creature away. I picked it up and laid it safely in the bushes."

"Later, after I touched my face, I felt some itching. That lead to cold sweats, faintness, and then my tongue swelled. I could hardly breathe, and I went into full anaphylactic shock – unconscious. Naomi called an ambulance. The paramedics jabbed me with adrenaline. I came around. They drove me away, and I spent a night in hospital with more injections and a drip. I found out later the poison in the toad's skin can cause severe allergic reactions in some vulnerable old folk and young children."

"We know how powerful toad pox can be. We use it in some of our potions. Do not worry. We will remember what you have said when we offer you anything. Please wait."

She flew high into the oak canopy and returned five minutes later.

She placed a pennywort leaf on the arm of the chair. She said, "Stop taking the pills I mentioned. If you come to see us every day and take this honey, you will become stronger. The poisons will begin to pass from your body. The cancers will retreat. All that is broken will slowly mend. The good health you have lost will return to you."

I took the honey offering. It tasted even better than the first time. She looked deep into my eyes and said, "Every day, Thomas."

I felt elated, like a butterfly broken free of its pupa. I returned to the house so quickly I hardly noticed the journey.

I gave the pennywort leaf to Joe's Faerie.

I burst into the kitchen. "Nay, I've been thinking. I've decided!" I said, a little too loudly. I softened my voice. "I'm coming off those damned pills."

"What?" She said, "Your heart pills?"

"Yes, and the anti-depressants. No more poison drugs for me."

She looked as if she didn't recognise me.

"Are you mad, Tom?" She said.

"No." I said, "I'm finished with all that. I've had enough. They make me ill."

"You'll be worse off without them." She said.

This made me doubt a little. "Well, let's see." I said, "If I get worse, I'll go back on them."

"If you ask me, you're nuts! Away with your bloody Faeries! You be careful, Tom. Faeries are tricksy folk. They can mess with your mind."

"Well, they've led me up the garden path a few times!" I joked.

I've been to the Glen every day and taken Sapphire's honey concoction and I must say, I've felt better and better. My joints don't hurt so much. My muscles don't ache. Ditching the anti-depressants made me ratty at first, but I soon came back to my old self. I lost the need for drinking fine Irish whiskey and stayed sober and awake in the evenings on a few glasses of wine. Naomi says I've become healthier, fitter, and, most importantly, nicer to be with.

I feel my energy firing up as soon as I open my eyes each morning, and I can't wait to skip up the cliff to meet my Faerie friend and get my taste of honey.

Today, I asked Sapphire, "What's in the honey you give me every day?"

"Honey."

"Just honey? But you said the honey would make me better, and I must say I'm stronger, and I feel so much younger."

"No, I said taking the honey every day would help you get better. It wasn't the honey. It was you."

"I don't understand."

"Thomas, you are an addict."

"I did drink too much."

"That is true, but you are also addicted to your infirmities. You have let them take over until they have become a necessary part of you. You need them. You are addicted to sadness and regret for past thoughts, words and deeds. You are addicted to fears you have nurtured since your childhood – fears of being thought ignorant, of being tricked, fooled, or being an object of ridicule or disdain. You are addicted to your fear of the growing darkness in the world, which you believe only a few blessed or cursed others can see. You feel responsible for waking up the sleeping people to the fear of impending doom that is eating away at you. You have been enthusiastically committed to all these addictions. Now you need new ones."

"To take your honey, you climbed the cliff every day. You pushed your muscles and joints past their limits. You inhaled the fresh forest air. You regenerated your lungs and your heart pumped harder. Every day you soaked in the spirit and the vibrations of the forest. You absorbed its pollens, spores, and microbes. That is why you feel better."

"So you… tricked me." I said.

"We tested you and your capacity to heal yourself without drugs." She smiled mischievously. "Oh, the honey made from local pollen helped your hay fever. The rest was all you."

"Oh, you clever Faerie!" I thought.

"This is only the first phase in your recovery." Sapphire said, "Now that you are behaving like a living man and not like a dying man, we can move on to the Curing and actively treat your heart disease and your cancers."

"What do I have to do?"

"You must stop eating dead animals. It makes you smell like a rotting carcass."

"I didn't know that. I'm so sorry. How embarrassing!"

"It fills you with fats that clog your heart and carcinogenic poisons that strangle your guts. It also fills you with hidden guilt for the killing. This guilt manifests as a spiritual tumour growing in your conscience. Every time your teeth tear into animal flesh, you curse yourself for causing the death of a living beast. For every mouthful of flesh you swallow, you also swallow your pride and feed your guilt."

"From now, we will be infusing your daily honey with specially selected herbal essences."

From a pocket in her gossamer gown, Sapphire produced a glass tube.

"Your personal prescription." She held the glass phial above the leaf and squeezed out a drop of honey. "You now have Muckruth Root, Devil Berries, Blister Cress, Viper Spit, Gagliafrasse, Docklaurel, Shimmer Nut Oil, Thunderseed, Blood Anise, Cavern Rue, Common Hazel Moss and Stinky Mallow."

"These will further shrink your cancers, strengthen your heart, revive your liver, cleanse your blood, smooth out your roughened joints, strengthen your ligaments, rejuvenate your skin and sharpen your senses."

"I am truly grateful for your care." I said and took the honey.

Today I told Sapphire I was feeling twenty years younger.

"Yes," she said, "We are very pleased with you. You are healthier, stronger, and happier."

"Thanks to you." I said.

"We think you are now ready," She said.

"Ready for what?"

"Ready for the Truth."

"What do you mean?"

"It is time for you to learn more about us, more about yourself, about the Universe. It is time to learn what no living human knows about our people, our ways, our crafts, our arts, medicine, and science. It is time for us to answer all the questions you have inside your head."

"That's amazing. Thank you!" I said.

"You will learn of many wonders," She said, "but first, you must make the third promise."

I nodded.

"Usually if any Faerie village is discovered by even one human," Sapphire said, "we know that trouble will follow closely. We know that destruction, deliberate or accidental, will be inevitable, so we move on straight away."

"When we go, there will be no trace. Everything here will return to what it was, as if we were never here."

"Thomas, we let you see us, and you heard our voices. We shared our names, and we have made you well. You promised to keep us secret, and we know you will protect us from harm until the day you die. We trust you, Thomas, and so we decided we will stay in this place, despite your discovery. We hope to stay until your last Earth days. We will protect you and your family. We will share our lives and lore with you."

I said, "I have made two promises. I am ready for another."

Sapphire said. "Thomas, we trust that you will constantly strive to be discrete and protect us. But you might one day expose us accidentally. It might be just a slip of the tongue when you talk to a friend."

"The safety of everyone in our village is dependent upon your vigilance. So, before we reveal everything, you must make your life dependent on keeping your promises."

"What do you mean?"

"Will you promise now, that if you, by will, or by accident, expose what you already know about us, or what you learn from us in future, or, if you put us in any danger…"

"I would never do that." I protested.

"… knowingly, or in error. Then you will willingly take a drop of honey, flavoured with toad pox. Will you promise that?"

I was stunned. "You know that would kill me?"

"Yes, we know."

"You know my tongue would swell. I would choke to

death?"

"As long as you keep your promises, you will live well, as you do now, and you will learn all you wish to know."

I fell silent. I considered her request.

"Sapphire," I said, "before I met you, I was feeling old and tired and sad. If you had asked me then to place my life in your hands, I might have quickly agreed, since I had so little to lose, but now I have everything to live for."

"Yes, and everything to learn and pass to your granddaughter."

"May I have time to think about it?" I asked, gingerly.

"Of course, Thomas, it is a big decision. Whatever you decide, we will continue to be friends. We will keep you well, and we will protect each other, but we will not be able to share our most secret of secrets. Please take as long as you need to decide, and then tell me if you wish to make your third promise."

"Thank you. I will."

"While you are deciding, please take this."

Sapphire handed me an exquisite wooden sphere.

It was made of dark wood, like cherry. It was the size of a tennis ball, perfectly round and polished impossibly smooth. I could see from a fine line around the middle that it was made in two halves. I glanced at Sapphire. She nodded. I gently twisted them apart. One half was a hollowed lid no thicker, but much stronger, than an eggshell. The other was a solid hemisphere with six cylindrical pegs inserted in a circle.

"I've never seen such craftsmanship as this." I said.

"I thought you would appreciate it, Thomas."

"I was a carpenter. I used to make fine furniture, until my hands and arms grew too weak. Now I just make puzzle boxes for my friends. I give one to Willow each year. Each one more complex than the last. She always figures them out. But I could never make anything as exquisite as this."

From three of the pegs sprouted what looked like sprays of fine hair. It was Sapphire's hair. It was red and gold, and the colours flickered like flames. I pulled out one of the sprouting pegs. It was a tiny vase turned from the wood, with the hair fixed into a finely drilled central tube. At the bottom of the peg, another hole was drilled at right angles, big enough to take a string.

She gestured to show it was for hanging around the neck.

"Each amulet contains a part of our Faerie body. That is our gift for you, your wife and your granddaughter to keep as your own, whatever you decide to do now. So long as you carry these charms with you, wherever you go, we will be better able to protect you. If you wish, you may each return the gift, with locks of your own hair."

"Thank you. We will gladly return your kind gift."

"And you will make your decision."

I nodded.

I walked home slowly. I felt weighed down with confusion and doubt.

I found Naomi waiting for me on the terrace.

"What's wrong, Tom?" she asked.

"Oh, I'm just a little tired, Nay" I lied.

"Well, let's do something to cheer you up. How about we use that fondue set Rolly and Gem gave us for Christmas? I've got some Cheddar and Gruyère, and there's fuel included with the burner. It'll be fun to try something new. Come on, Tom, let's have a cheesy dip."

"No, thank you, darling. I'm really not in the mood," I said.

"Or I could make you a nice Toad in the Hole?"

"No, thanks. I just want to sit here in peace for a while."

Naomi raised her eyebrows and gave me a knowing look. "Bad memories, Tom?"

I shook my head.

"Or have those Faeries been toying with you? I've told you before, they can be tricksy. Mother said they can be wilful, capricious child-spirits or much worse! They can bring death, like the Banshee. They came like fearsome ghouls, to wail and keen outside the houses of the sick. They frighten them so much they'd have heart attacks and die."

"But these Faeries aren't like that. They're beautiful people," I said.

"Faeries may appear beautiful, like the Leanan Sidhe. She was a beautiful vampire who seduced Irish men, poets and musicians. She inspired the best of their work, but eventually, they paid for it with their life-blood," Naomi said.

"That's just a story. These Faeries are real and they're not malicious at all." I said.

"There may be some good fairies, but even they can be easily offended. It wouldn't be good to be on their bad side or disappoint them. They might grant your wishes or be your friends for a while, but if you offend them or disappoint them, you could be in deep trouble."

"Mother told us about Faeries who drowned people or made them dance night and day until they wasted away. They could blight people's crops or curse them into madness, sickness, or death."

"Mother told me once, my grandmother, Niamh, was taken by the Faeries from her first home."

I shook my head in disbelief.

"Shake your head all you want, Tom Archer, but one thing my mother always said was to never make a bargain with the Fae Folk. If you break it, they will break you," Naomi stomped off into the house.

I sat on the terrace, nursed a Guinness and watched the river

Every twenty minutes, the paddle wheels of the Higher Ferry, would splash to shore, and the wooden prowl would judder up the slipway. At low tide, it would come to rest about ninety yards down the slip. Now, at high tide, it stopped just forty yards from the house.

Colin the ferryman saw me cradling my beer and called up, "Hey, Tom, mine's a pint of lager." I'd normally return a witty response to Colin's quips, but now all I could muster was "Cheers, Mate!"

I sat by the river until dusk, when the last yachts and motorboats tied up for the night at the Marina. I watched on into darkness. The twinkling lights of Dartmouth reflected in zigzags across the water.

From the navy pontoons in Old Mill Creek, seals cried a lament for their lost children and ancestors. The ferry gates clanged open and closed. St. Saviours church chimed eleven.

Naomi was used to what she called my 'downtimes' and she kindly left me to it. At eleven thirty, the ferry stopped and moored up on the far side of the river. All waterborne movement ceased.

The owls hooted in the woods, bats flitted above my head and mice rustled in the bushes. At midnight, the Naval College bell chimed eight bells for the end of the sailors' First Watch and the start of the Middle Watch.

But this was my Black Watch. I'd never felt so alone. My whole life teetered on the cliff edge at that moment. Should I make the third promise and learn of wonders no human could imagine? Should I refuse and be content with my new-found good health and a limited but delightful friendship with my Faerie friend?

Is Sapphire's promise of Faerie wisdom worth risking my life? Should I make such a bargain with a Faerie?

It would be easy for them to carry out the threat behind the promise. If they ever think I've put them in danger, they only have to lace my daily gift of honey and herbal healing with a drop of toad pox. Then, hives, swollen tongue, choking, asphyxiation, death – all within minutes.

Could it be a trick? Sapphire had kind-of tricked me before, implying that the honey made me feel stronger and fitter, when it was the exercise of climbing the cliff every day to take the honey that did it.

But... perhaps they were just being reasonable. If they were accidentally exposed, curious tourists would swarm into the Hoodown Woods. They would trample over their village. They would bring their kids Faerie hunting, with their crab nets and plastic buckets. Scientists would come from the universities with their butterfly nets and Kilner jars to trap specimens. Television companies would come to tape a jokey ending to the news, about Faeries at the bottom of an old fool's garden.

Sapphire was only asking me to be extra careful to keep the promises I've already made. A promise is a promise. Nothing has changed.

I can do this.

This morning I climbed the path to meet Sapphire. She was waiting in the centre of the Glen, surrounded by dozens of her Faerie Folk, who glittered in the sunlight.

I handed her the wooden sphere, with three amulets charged with locks of our hair. Each was gifted willingly. I called Willow, and she agreed, directing me to the hairbrush in the travel box she always left with us. It was under her holiday toothbrush and cuddly rabbit.

I'd shown Naomi the sphere and told her where it came from and what it meant. She said, "You're serious about this Faerie stuff, Tom. Are you sure this isn't all just in your imagination?"

I said. "I didn't imagine this." She took the sphere and

examined it carefully.

She nodded. "No furniture maker could make this." She said, "Not even you. But I'm not sure it's a good idea. Mother once said, if a witch gets one lock of your hair, she can weave it into a Cailleach – a corn doll. Then the hag can stick pins in it to make you ill."

"The Faeries aren't witches, Nay." I said.

"You'd better be sure of that." She said.

Naomi cut a lock of her hair and one of mine and did the fiddly job of inserting the hair into the pegs.

Later, when I handed the sphere to Sapphire. She said: "We thank you, Thomas and your family, for your gifts. Do you wish to make the third promise?"

I took a deep breath and said, "I promise that I will willingly take the pox of the toad if I ever, by accident or design, fail to keep my promises and put you in peril."

I heard a great swell of Faerie voices. It was a choral symphony that floated to the treetops. Faeries joined hands and danced, they spun and tumbled in the air. They swarmed around Sapphire and me in a circle of sparkling wings.

I don't know how long this celebration lasted. Time seemed to stretch beyond my understanding, but it eventually subsided.

Sapphire spoke into the silence of the forest, "Thomas,

this day we welcome you into the world of Faerie. From this day, you will be known as Thomas ToadMaster."

"From tomorrow, we will teach you whatever you wish to learn. We will keep no secrets from you. We will protect you and your family. At the end of your Earth time, you will move on and so will we. You will pass your learning to your granddaughter, Willow, so that she may, in her time, pass it down all the human ages."

"Thank you." I said. I could only smile the biggest, stupidest smile.

A dozen Faeries flew into the tree and returned carrying between them a heavy load.

"We give you the Journal." Sapphire said, grandly gesturing to the book as they dropped it into my hands.

It was five inches wide by seven long, and an inch thick. It was bound in a cover, of rusty-brown polished leather, exquisitely inlaid with fine veins of a smooth red-gold velvety material, the colours of which flickered like Sapphire's flaming hair. The venous lines were so furry, it was impossible not to stroke them. I felt a tingle run through my fingers. The veins snaked across the cover morphing into images of butterflies, bees, vines, then lilies, leaves of oak, hazel, and sycamore. All the beings of the forest were here in this book.

"The leather is sung from the leaves of Hedera Helix, the

ivy."

"Sung?" I asked.

"You will learn about Singing." She said. "The ivy, although common, is special. We call it Hidey Vine because it keeps our Faerie places covered and secret, and it will help keep the Journal secret. The veins are sung from the tender young leaves of Verbascum Thapsus, the mullein. We call it the Hare's Beard. Each time you touch it, the veins will dance and pass the power of the Forest through your fingers."

I opened the front cover to reveal the first page, in the finest, smoothest pale yellow vellum.

"The pages are sung from cowslip petals. You used to call it the Faerie Cup, but we do not use it for drinking. The Prime Rose can, however, be used to open treasure chests and even split rocks to reveal hidden treasure. In the Journal it will help keep our secrets safe from those who should not see them."

In the centre of the page, in the most beautiful flowing Faerie hand, was the inscription:

A True and Faithful Record
From the Hand of Thomas Archer ToadMaster
of Kingswear, Devon, England
Signed in His Own Blood:

And Witnessed by
Sapphire Silverwings of Hoodown Woods:

_____

On This Day:

_____

Sapphire, produced a wren's feather. She stroked the point over the back of my hand and without breaking the skin, the quill filled with blood. She handed me the quill and I carefully signed my name on the line. She waved her right hand over the page and her name appeared. She completed the date: 6th June 1986.

"Our promises are made." Sapphire said, and the faeries handed me a glass jar. It was the size of a pear, shaped like a water droplet with a flat bottom. Sapphire demonstrated the screw-on glass stopper. The jar was full of black liquid.

"We made this ink from crushed oak gall, with a little gum aarabic from the acacia for thickening, and a dash of green vitriol to deepen the brown to black. Please use this ink and nothing else. It will bind your words to the page forever. It has other properties you will discover. You must write only with your own fountain pen."

When I returned home I placed the Journal and ink, on the kitchen table while I removed my boots.

"What's that?" Naomi asked, and before I could stop her,

she reached over and picked up the book.

"Beautiful cover." She said, running her fingers over the velvety veins. She shivered slightly. "Haven't seen work like this for a long time."

"No, nor me. Never, in fact." I said.

"Mother had such a book as this, a gift from my grandmother, Niamh."

"The Faeries gave it to me." I said nervously. "They want me to write about them."

"Tom, you old kidder. You can't write a bloody shopping list. I bet you got it in the Air Ambulance shop and paid far too much for it."

"Nay, will you come with me and meet them?"

"Hmm. You know I'm not at all keen." She said.

7

Sapphire greeted me this morning with all her Faerie folk. They hovered behind her, sang a song about the True World of Faerie, and danced a Celtic jig.

When Sapphire spoke, they dispersed into their tree.

"Welcome, Thomas ToadMaster, to the true world of Faerie. What do you wish to learn?"

I had been waiting for this moment for many weeks. I was so excited I could hardly breathe.

I said, "Will you tell me… all about Faerie life?"

"That would take thousands of years, Thomas. We have been here a long time. It would be better if you ask specific questions.

"I have a million questions. I don't know where to start."

"No matter where you start. It will all come together."

"OK, then… The wooden sphere with the amulets. I have never seen wood, crafted like that, so perfectly, so smooth. Did you make that?"

"That's a good place to start, Thomas, for you will learn how we relate to the material world. Let me show you. Pass me a log."

I picked a log from the forest floor, about 4 inches in diameter and 18 inches long. I laid it before her. She hovered above the log. I could hear an ultra-high-pitched sound. It was like the tinnitus ring you get after a hearing a very loud bang.

I could see a pencil-thin line circling the log. It began to glow orange and pulse until, after a few seconds, the log split in two. There was a perfectly flat cut. So smooth, it appeared polished.

Then she made a cut three inches away and produced a disk. I reached for it. The cut surfaces were perfectly smooth and perfectly parallel.

"How did you cut it so flat, so fine? "

"I did not cut. I sang it into shape. We call it the Singing. Watch…"

She gestured to me to place it down. I put it flat on the grass between us. She hovered above the disk and sang a high-pitched whistle.

In the middle, a small circle of wood shimmered. The circle grew to an inch diameter and its surface appeared to become liquid. She changed her note, sliding it deeper. The liquid wood evaporated to reveal a cylinder an inch deep, perfectly smooth and polished.

"There" she said, "A holder for your bedside candle. Please take it to Naomi as our gift."

I was entranced, shocked. "How?"

"We can soften the wood, turn it to jelly or liquid or make it evaporate. We can do this with any earthly material – wood, stone, metal. We have seen you with your saws, drills, chisels, files, and hammers. You attack things with other things and slowly the harder wears the softer away. Very noisy, dusty, clumsy and slow. We just… sing."

"To make bigger things, we sing together. We can sing tunnels through rocks, make chambers in the heartwood of trees."

She flew before my face and said, "Sit down, close your eyes and follow me."

I closed my eyes and found myself in a huge wooden chamber. The roof was a perfect parabolic curve. The surface was seamless and perfectly smooth like a turned and polished bowl, studded with thousands of tiny lights.

The floor of the chamber was perfectly level, flat, and shining, reflecting the network of lights above.

"How do the lights work?"

"We sing light tubes. They go up through the heartwood and into the top branches. They gather the sunlight or the moonlight, and it bounces from the tube walls and multiplies until it shines bright all the way to here."

Leading from the walls there were perfectly cylindrical tunnels. Around the entrance to each tunnel were beautiful reliefs. Sinuous vines, fruits, faerie forms, more skilled and beautiful than any human hand could ever make.

"It's like Art Nouveau!" I breathed.

"It is Art Nouveau."

"Did you learn this from humans?"

"The humans learned from us."

"I wish I could create such beauty."

"Perhaps you could, Thomas. Will you show me one of your puzzle boxes?"

"Of course."

I suddenly became conscious that we were talking inside a

tree and that was impossible.

"Might I ask where we are?" I said.

"Look over there." She pointed to one wall of the chamber. As I turned to follow her, the wall shimmered to transparency. I saw, far below us, an old man dozing in a fisherman's chair."

"Sapphire," I said, "Is this real or am I dreaming?"

Sapphire asked, "Are you dreaming?"

"It doesn't feel like a dream. I've had dreams before when I suddenly realise I'm dreaming. I walk off a roof and I don't fall, just fly down. Then I know I'm dreaming, so I search for interesting places to fly. But I've never been able to talk to someone I met in a dream about a dream while I'm still in the dream."

"So," Sapphire asked again, "are you dreaming?"

Eight bells. End of the First Watch. I can't sleep.

Today I flew inside an oak tree with a Faerie. Tonight I lay in my bed thinking. *That's not possible. It must have been a dream. I must've fallen asleep in the sunshine and drifted off.*

But I know it wasn't a dream.

When I dream, I wake up and, try as I may, I can't remember what happened. I might have a vague image of being in a strange house, but I can't recall what it looked like. I can only see drifting images, that constantly change. I can't remember someone's face from a dream or words from a conversation.

Yet, I remember everything from my flight inside the tree – its scent, the feel of the sinuous forms in the Art Nouveau woodwork, Sapphire's face, her eyes and every word she said.

And Sapphire gave me a real candleholder to bring home.

I didn't dream that. I gave it to Naomi and told her it's a gift from the Faeries. She didn't ask if it was real. She said it was beautifully made.

Naomi said, "My grandmother had pieces, polished very smooth, just like this."

She placed it on her bedside table.

It's not a dream.

Tomorrow I will take one of my pieces to show Sapphire.

I was nervous to show Sapphire my clumsy work, having seen and touched the exquisite objects her Faerie Sisters could sing from wood. I expected my puzzle box would appear crude.

This box was in the form of a pencil case. I was making it for Willow's next birthday. It was of Oak with inset Mahogany framing the edges. I'd inlaid diamond-shaped veneer cuttings of contrasting cedar and mahogany. There was no visible lid. The box was designed to appear solid.

Sapphire hovered around it, studying every square inch.

"It is very well-made, Thomas, considering the crude tools you have to use. Show me how you open it."

I pressed a cedar diamond in the centre of each end. A mahogany diamond popped up in the middle of the top of the box. I twisted it on a hidden pin and out popped a cedar diamond on the underside. I pressed both raised diamonds. A hidden spring expanded with a satisfying "Boinnggg!" The top of the box flipped open on a hidden hinge at the back. The divide zigzagged along the diamond edges around the horizontal centre line of the box, so when open, it looked like the mouth of a shark. Inside was a collection of coloured pencils.

Sapphire clapped and shrieked, just as Willow would have

done.

"It's wonderful!." She exclaimed.

"I made it for Willow, but may I gift it to you?" I asked.

"Oh no. The gift must go to the one it was made for. But you can, if you wish, make another such box in which you can hide the Journal from unwelcome eyes."

"I would love to do that." I said.

"We need you to make it so complex that only you and young Willow will ever be able to open it." Sapphire said. "It will be our gift to Willow and to each other. Will you do that, Thomas?"

"Might take a while." I said.

I asked Sapphire, "So, you can sing wood into shape. What else can you sing?"

"Close your eyes. Follow me." She said.

I again found myself inside the tree, flying with Sapphire through a tunnel into a small chamber. Six fairies hovered in a circle around a perfect cylinder sung from a slab of wood. In the centre of this plinth, a flat amoebic blob of what looked like gold. They sang in harmony, and the blob formed into a perfectly circular disk, and curled up into a bowl. They sang a complex fugue with six separate vocal parts, weaving spiralling melodies and rich harmonies. As they sang, the surface of the gold shivered and vibrated. When they stopped, the bowl was exquisitely figured with lacy filigree reliefs and perforations, creating grapevines, butterflies, spiders in delicate webs of gold filament.

"We have no need for your furnaces, tools, or moulds when we can sing a picture in a rock, a tree, or a plate of gold."

"I could never, in a million years, imagine this was possible." I said.

"Did you never wonder why singing evolved and survived in the Universe, if it was only for entertainment? Everything is formed from song. It was you who invented straight lines and right angles and joints because that is how your tools make forms. We sing everything into shape."

"May I ask something else?"

"Of course, Thomas, ask whatever you wish."

"Well, where do you find the gold?"

"We sing it, of course, Come with me."

We floated through a maze of tunnels to a new chamber.

"This is where we do the Changing, We can make almost anything from natural earth."

Five Faeries threw clods of earth into a large wooden crucible. They stood in a pentagon equally spaced around the bowl and sang.

The earth appeared to melt and bubble as if boiling. Then it settled into what looked like a grey lump of iron. More singing, and it changed to the colour of copper.

"The whole of the Universe is made of energy – particles and waves. It is all music! We learned to sing it." Sapphire said.

"So… the vibration in the notes and the harmonic resonance – that's what changes the structure of the material?" I asked.

"You could put it that way. Watch, Thomas."

The three Faeries sang a higher note, and the copper transformed into gold.

"Is it real gold?" I asked.

"Of course, although it is purer than your gold."

"It's like alchemy." I said.

"No, not at all. We showed your Greek and Egyptian ancestors how we sing gold from the earth. But they did not understand it was a process of physics, of vibration. They could only conceive of making it by manipulating their four elements: Earth, Air, Fire and Water. They focussed on the chemistry. So try as they may, they could never make it work. But maybe that was for the best." She said, " Some of your predecessors lusted after rarity, riches, and too much home-made gold would have destroyed them. We just make gold for its beauty and purity."

I asked, "What do you do with the gold treasures you make?"

Sapphire said, "We use them ourselves, of course, when we have special banquets to celebrate, and we give them to other Faerie villages."

"You trade them?" I asked.

"We call it the Gifting." Sapphire said, "It's not the same as your trade or even barter. Exchanged gifts do not need to have equivalent value. You see, everyone has something to give, which, to them, is as precious as a gold dish. It might be a jar of honey mead that took three years to mature, or a story of an ancient Faerie adventure, or a song for calming bees or setting broken bones."

"We give what we can create or discover, and our friends return the gift with something they create or discover. Our gift of a gold dish to the *Xxxxx Beach Faeries might be returned with a dozen dogfish egg sacks, that we can use for preserving precious herbal seeds. The *Xxxxx Hill Faeries might gift a score of rare white bluebell bulbs. The *Xxxxx Rock Faeries might gift a song for charming seals or cormorants ."

[*Xxxxx - Place names have been obscured to protect the location of other local Faerie villages. — Willow Archer]

"I understand." I said, "That doesn't quite work in human economics."

"Oh it does sometimes." Sapphire said, "You know that Willow cannot make a puzzle box in return for your gift, but you know that moment of her delight when she opens it, is worth more than a puzzle box made of gold."

I returned home with my head full of wonder. What I had seen was totally impossible, but I knew it was all real. No dream or illusion. It was real. That is how the material world behaves if you know how to sing it into resonance.

I tried to tell Naomi what I'd found out, but I think she'd grown weary of my talk about Faeries. She made tea and dropped three sugars in mine. "One for you. One for me. One for little Daisy Lee. Don't let it go cold." She went back to her painting.

Today, as I waited for Sapphire, I noticed a spider had spun a web across the dark opening to the village. When Sapphire flew out, she passed through the web without breaking it.

When she saw the question on my face, she said, "We have a special relationship with spiders. We have been friends with them for millennia. We taught them how to weave interference patterns in their webs that reflect ultraviolet light and attract more flies. They make fresh webs each day and gift us yesterday's webs. We collect them at night."

"What do you use them for?"

"Follow." She said, and flew me into the tree to a new

chamber. The ceiling was flared like the bell of a trumpet that narrowed into a tube and disappeared up towards the top of the tree.

Two fairies took a cotton-wool bundle of rough gossamer from a basket. They placed it in the centre of the chamber and sang a tone that set the gossamer ball spinning. As they raised the pitch, the gossamer was pulled into a fine thread, so light it drifted in long, almost invisible strands into the trumpet bell and away up into the chimney.

Then they sang another tone into the flue. It resonated deeply like a church organ pipe, and translucent sheets of fabric fluttered down like leaves and landed in a pile. They lifted each one carefully and draped them over a gossamer line. They were shaped into cloaks, like the one Sapphire wore. The Faeries sang another tone, and down floated a dozen little hammocks with silky rope ties at each end.

Another two Faeries were stuffing bundles of gossamer into cylindrical moulds of polished wood. When they sang, the gossamer mass spun faster and faster and coated the sides of the moulds. They changed the pitch and the cloudy gossamer became transparent. The Faeries reached in and pulled out fine drinking glasses, which they pinged with their fingernails to show they rang perfectly.

"Gossamer glass?" I said, not believing what I had just seen.

"Yes. We can also make fine flexible glass, like your plastic sheeting. We can sing it opaque, any colour you choose. We can make super-transparent glass that reflects no light at all and use it as an invisible barrier to seal off a space."

"We can make almost anything from gossamer," Sapphire said, "lace, string, rope, nets. If we can think it, we can make it. Some Faeries have created gossamer glass cities, castles, which reflect perfectly the forest or hills around them, making their villages and all within them, totally invisible."

"We can make elastic glass. Can you imagine what you could do with that?"

"Er…"

"Come, Thomas."

I followed her to a chamber with a domed roof. Faeries were flying near the ceiling and dropping acorns. I ducked and covered my head with my arms. But no acorns fell around me or hit the floor. I looked up gingerly.

The acorns fell and stopped mid-air and bounced back to the Faeries, who made a game of catching them.

"That is elastic gossamer glass."

"It's like transparent rubber." I said.

"Yes and very hard to break. It is tougher than steel. If you used it in a window, you could run at it as fast as you like. It would absorb your energy and gently bounce you back. Or we can tune the elasticity to add speed to the bounce, even double it. If you run into a sheet of super elastic gossamer, it could push you back twice as fast."

"Can you teach me to sing gossamer?" I joked.

"That would take more than fifty human lifetimes."

That night I dreamed I invented an Exponential Gossamer Accelerator. I imagined a square-sectioned tube, about ten inches long, with walls of super-elastic gossamer. The tube lay horizontal on my kitchen table. I had a metal pipe pierced into the tube at each end, at just one degree from vertical.

I dropped a steel ball bearing down the entry pipe at two miles an hour. It hit the bottom wall of the tube and bounced up, like light from a mirror. It hit the top wall at twice the speed. It continued to bounce between the walls, doubling speed at each bounce: 2... 4... 8... 16... 32 miles per hour. After just fifteen bounces, it was travelling at 64,000 miles per hour.

I was so excited I woke myself up. I slipped out of bed, and being careful not to wake Naomi, I tip-toed to my desk. I took my electronic calculator and worked out that, after twenty-nine bounces, the ball would be travelling at 536,870,912 miles per hour. One more bounce and it would exceed the speed of light!

If I positioned the escape pipe in just the right place, the ball would bounce out, burst through our stone cottage walls and fly off into space.

I grabbed my notebook and designed a version of the accelerator that could launch full-size space rockets. You can see the *drawing below.

The rocket is embedded in a spherical shell. It's then dropped into a huge accelerator, bounced up to speed and then shot beyond the Earth's gravitation field. The shell then falls away, and the rocket continues to space powered only by small jets.

Just think of the massive saving in fuel, in rocket size and weight. There would be no ignition fireball, no atmospheric pollution, and the launch would even be silent. Just think how that could accelerate our exploration of space and Human colonisation of other planets!

Maybe I should write to NASA and tell them about it! They might laugh, or they might... Hmm! They might think it would be a great way to silently launch nuclear-armed rockets to Russia with no jet burn to be detected by heat-seeking defence satellites. Perhaps I won't tell them.

Here's my *drawing anyway.

[*Thomas inserted his notebook page into the Journal. His detailed drawing has been omitted to protect the world from nuclear Armageddon. — Willow Archer]

I noticed whenever Sapphire talked to me, there was more than words in my head. I had flashes of images, smells, hints of memories too.

Today I asked her what was happening.

"Thomas, we can communicate with you in many ways. Not just by words travelling through the air. Are you ready for this?"

"Hello, Thomas."

I heard someone very close by. I spun around to see who was talking. But the sound was inside my head, like listening to a taped story through the Walkman headphones.

I looked at Sapphire, questioning.

She nodded and smiled.

"Yes, it's me, Thomas." She said without speaking.

"You're talking inside my head?"

"Yes, and you can now talk back inside your head. Just think what you want to say."

"Like this." I thought.

"Just like that." She thought back.

"Or you can imagine something you want to show me, like this…"

I found myself on the beach at Sugary Cove, where some of her Faerie cousins were flitting about at the water's edge collecting tiny carnelian gemstones.

"Or, you can remember something, and we will both live through it. Like this…"

I was looking from a twig in the Oak tree. I saw Willow skipping up the cliff, her dove fluttering above her. She suddenly froze, turned and looked straight at me, or was it at Sapphire? Willow clapped her hands to her cheeks, sucked in a deep breath and stretched her eyes wide. "It's a Faerie!" Willow gasped, transfixed by what she saw.

"That's the moment your granddaughter spotted me." Sapphire thought.

"That's telepathy!" I said.

"Now, Thomas, we can speak when we cannot speak."

This morning I was drinking tea on the terrace, listening to the Naval College band practising for the cadets' Passing Out Parade, when their proud parents come to see them marching on the parade ground.

"Heart of oak are our ships, jolly tars are our men,
we always are ready; Steady, boys, steady!
We'll fight, and we'll conquer again and again."

I watched the wind paint its patterns on the river, when a tiny mouse appeared from the far end of the terrace wall. It walked slowly towards me until it was less than two feet away. I was about to shoo it off, before Naomi saw it – she hates rodents – but I hesitated. It was such a beautiful creature. The mouse sat on the wall and stared at me for a moment, then squeaked and ran back the way it came.

I realised later that Sapphire had sent the mouse as a clue to what was about to happen.

I climbed to the Glen and sat in my chair waiting for Sapphire to appear.

Under the fallen boughs I caught a dark movement. As my eyes accustomed to the gloom, it looked like the earth under the logs was boiling. Brown bubbles were popping up and sliding wildly across the soil. Concentrating harder, I saw the bubbles were hairy. It was a swarm of mice, thousands of them running in every direction, spilling over each other.

The swarm suddenly froze and all their snouts turned to me. I was terrified as they flowed like a tsunami out from the shadows and over the grass in my direction. I'd just found one squeaking mouse charming, but thousands of mice all chirping and squeaking together combined to a terrifying scream.

I jumped from the chair and started to run, when the screaming suddenly stopped and I heard a chorus of laughing voices.

When I looked back, the mice had sprouted wings. They had become a cloud of Faeries, bobbing and twisting and weaving in a dance above my head.

Sapphire appeared before me, grinning. "We thought you might like to witness a Seeming. I hope we didn't scare you."

"Well, actually, I was terrified!" I gasped, "But thank you for the demonstration." I calmed down a little. "You can change into mice? That's fantastic!"

"We don't really change, we just seem to be different. It can be useful if we need to confuse a predator or if we want to go somewhere in disguise."

"Oh, you clever Faerie!" I thought. Sapphire smiled.

"Mice. What else can you do?" I said aloud.

"We can morph into birds, frogs, or your favourites, toads. For big animals, we can make a swarm in the creature's shape. We can do rabbits, badgers, deer, even horses. That is hard work. We can only keep it up for a few minutes, although that is usually enough to bamboozle a human."

"Is it like hypnosis? Do I see what I expect to see? Or do you really change shape? Is the Seeming an illusion."

"It is." Sapphire said.

"And... since we met, you seem to me like a tiny human with wings. Is that an illusion? Do I see what I want to see, a storybook Faerie, I can relate to?"

"Thomas, your whole world is what you want to see. Your world is not what is. There is no *is*. There is only what you dream. We are part of your dream. You see us, as you wish to see us."

"So, you're not humans or dragonflies or toads or any kind of animal?"

"That is true, Thomas."

"Then, What are you?"

"I think you already know." She said.

"You're Spirit." I said.

Sapphire nodded.

8

When I saw Sapphire today, I said, "I understand you are spirits and you have lived many thousands of years. Will you tell me where you came from?"

Sapphire took a deep breath, like one embarking on an impossible task. "I will try." She said.

She hesitated, and I could feel a tickling deep inside my head.

I put my hand to the back of my head. "What was that?" I said.

"I was exploring your memory to find something you know which would help me explain from your perspective."

"Hold on!" I said, alarmed, "You can read my mind?"

"Only what you allow me to read." She said.

"Oh… OK, but it tickles," I said, "and it makes me…" I sneezed.

"It is meant to, so you know when it is happening."

"Well, what did you find?" I asked.

"You know about the Dreamtime."

"The Aboriginal Dreamtime?" I said.

"Yes, so you can think of us as Spirits of the Dreamtime." Sapphire said.

"When the first humans thought about Nature, they believed She was their enemy. Natural forces killed people with floods, or starved them with droughts. Spiders and snakes poisoned them. They believed there were evil spirits inside the weather, the animals, and the rocks, all determined to destroy them."

"They tried to hunt the spirits down and kill them, but they found they could not be killed. The storms and the snakes always came back. So, they tried to appease the spirits by making gifts. They sacrificed their lambs and even their babies to please the weather spirits. But still the storms and droughts came."

"The First Nations people of Australia realised if they understood the spirits better, they could learn to share the Earth with them in peace and plenty. So, they invented a new story. The story of The Dreamtime and for over 60,000 years, they passed that story down through all their generations. It is the foundation of their religion, culture, and their lives."

"They believe the Dreamtime creation started in the beginning and continues now and is never-ending. They believe the land they occupy was once free of form, vacuous, barren. In the Dreamtime, the sky above, the mountains, hills, rivers, plants and all lifeforms, were dreamed into existence by the spirits."

"The spirits then disappeared from the sight of humans, but they continued to dream the world. They still observe and influence human life. Some spirits went into the sky as heavenly bodies – the Planets and the Stars that steer life on Earth, the Tides, the Seasons. Some became natural forces –

the Wind, Rain, Thunder, and Lightning. Each species of plant and animal had its own spirit guide and spirits inhabited all earth forms – rivers, hills, plains, and rocks."

"The Aboriginals believe that some spirits, like the Faeries, stayed visible, but in hiding, close to the humans, to observe and help them. They lived in secret places – rock crevices, hollow trees and water holes."

"At a certain level, Thomas, all of this is true. We Faeries chose our body form, like small humans the size of insects, so we could blend into your dreamworld. We can enter into other creatures when we wish, the spiders on your ceilings, the wild birds you feed, your cows, your pet cats and dogs, your vermin, mice and cockroaches. In this way, we can always be close to you. We can watch over you without being noticed, and we can guide you with the Whispering."

"That is astonishing and beautiful." I said.

Last night, I hardly slept a wink. My brain was buzzing. Sapphire had said she was a Spirit of the Dreamtime. This was a lot for me to take in. I have always been sceptical of anything to do with the spirit world – God, the Angels, the Devil and Faeries.

Yes, I go to church sometimes, and I enjoy the sense of sanctuary, peace, and continuity I feel in the building and traditions. I sing along with hymns and I say the prayers. I go to weddings, funerals, and christenings. I do all that for Naomi and the children, but I never actually believed all that spiritual stuff.

Now I'm seeing Faeries! I talk to them. I do telepathy with them. I have seen with my own eyes and held in my hands, the wonderful things they can make. I am bewildered by it all.

I'm a practical man. I work in wood. Yes, I can understand how resonating harmonies from notes sung at high frequencies could possibly cut and shape wood or metal. That sounds like physics. But my brain is wrestling with the existence, in my garden, of spirits from the ancient Dreamtime.

The next time we met, I asked Sapphire, "Will you tell me more about the world of spirits?"

"Ask your questions, Thomas."

"Well, please forgive me, but I never believed that spirits existed."

"Thomas, first, you do not have to believe we are spirit for us to be spirit. If you were a worm living under the ground. You would not believe the sky existed. Yet, it does. We do not need your belief."

"I understand." I said.

"Second thing, Thomas, if you know something, then you do not have to believe it. You only have to believe in things you do not see, hear, touch or know. But, you know us. You see us. You speak with us. So do not worry about believing in us."

"Forgive me, Sapphire, but you might be just an old man's pathetic delusion." I said.

"Thomas, where is the candlestick I made for you."

"As you kindly suggested, I gave it to Naomi." I said.

"Does she like it?" Sapphire said.

"Yes, I did think about that. She loves it. She keeps it beside her bed. It's real, isn't it?"

"You are not a delusional old man." Sapphire said.

I asked Sapphire, "Will you tell me more? Are you a Spirit of the Earth?"

"We are here to care for life on Earth, but we are not of the Earth. We are Spirits of the Universe." She said.

I thought I might be getting ahead of myself, but I took a deep breath and asked, "So, can you tell me about the Universe?"

"That's a big question, Thomas. Perhaps you could ask something more specific?"

Embarrassed, I said, "Of course. Is there intelligent life out there?"

"Oh yes. The Universe is teeming with life." Sapphire said.

"Advanced life?"

"There is life at all stages of development."

"Are there any human-like species out there?"

"Oh, I thought you wanted to talk about *advanced* life." Sapphire said, with raised eyebrows and a wicked smile.

"You funny Faerie!" I joked, "I was thinking of other conscious beings with sophisticated civilisations."

"They are as common as pebbles on your beaches." She said.

"Do they ever visit Earth?"

"It has happened before."

"The Anunnaki?" I asked.

"Among others. They came to Earth when your prehistoric ancestors were simple hunter-gatherers. They taught you much, although much you have forgotten. They taught the Ancient Egyptians to sing rock to make their pyramids."

Now I felt like a schoolboy who had stumbled across the answer sheet to the end-of-term exam papers. Dare I take a peep? Dare I ask more?

I said, "People say they have seen spaceships, UFOs. Some say they've actually seen aliens."

"Those people mostly saw other residents of Earth. They live here, beside you.'

"You mean, in parallel dimensions?"

"Exactly," She said, "and in remote places in your dimension that you know little about."

"Do you watch over them?"

"No, they have their own Folk. We visit them sometimes. But our work is here."

"So, can you travel to other dimensions?"

"Yes, we do it every day, and we also go to other times. But we would not call it travelling, it is just a hop and a skip for us. You have seen me do it before."

"Have I?"

"Watch." She said.

Sapphire hovered above the log beside my chair, where I'd placed my coffee flask.

She looked at me, blinked and suddenly disappeared

"Where are you?" I said.

"Right here." She said, reappearing out of nothing. "I just hopped into another dimension, without moving in space. Now watch this."

She blinked and disappeared again.

"Where are you now?" I asked.

No answer.

I waited and watched and nothing happened. After five minutes, I assumed Sapphire had gone home to her Faerie village. Then she reappeared.

"Where did you go?" I asked.

"Nowhere." She said, "I was here."

"So what happened? You changed dimensions?"

"No. I was in your dimension. I just stepped five minutes into your future, and I have been waiting here for you to catch up."

"Marvellous!" I said, "And can you hop into the past?"

"Yes. We do, constantly. You see, for you, for your sanity, you think time runs in a straight line in one direction, from what you call the past to what you call the future. For us, past, present and future are all here now. We flit between them all day."

"What's that like?"

She hesitated, and I felt her exploring inside my head. I sneezed.

She said, "You sometimes trip in time without knowing."

"Really?"

"Have you ever walked into a room to get something and then forgotten what you came there for?"

"All the time."

"When you enter the new room, you forget why you were there because you actually flipped back to a time when you had not yet thought of the reason for going there."

"Er…"

She rummaged in my memories again.

"Have you ever forgotten whether you put sugar in your tea and added more, just in case. Then you taste the tea and find it is too sweet?"

"Well, yes."

"It is the same thing. You circled back in time to when

you had not yet sugared your tea, so you dropped some in. When you returned to your present, you had two lots of sugar."

"I see." I didn't.

"Do you ever have déjà vu when you think you have been here and done this before?"

"Oh yes."

"Well you have. Some while ago, you must have meandered forward to that time and place, and you did whatever you did in that future time. You saw who you saw. You said what you said. Then you wandered back in time to your present when that event had not yet happened. You then had to live second by second, hour by hour until you reached the time of the future event you had already experienced and that is when you thought 'This has happened before.'"

"Why can't we do it deliberately, like you, flip back and forth between dimensions and times?"

"Remember, Thomas, we are Spirits of the Universe. We exist beyond worlds, dimensions and times, so for us, it is easy to slide between them. You were created for this world, this dimension. Your bodies are complex physical communities with millions of microscopic life forms, all locked up in a thin boundary of human skin. Your existence is dependent upon bounded space and time as it manifests in this dimension. Without those boundaries, your dream of yourself as a separate entity, and your actual existence as a person, would evaporate and merge into everything."

"So, will we ever be able to travel in time or to parallel dimensions?" I asked.

"Not within your bodies."

"Outside our bodies?"

"The only way out of your physical bonds is by waking from your dream."

"Death?" I asked.

"Yes, or transcendence to the One." She said.

"Will you show me?" I asked.

"I will. Before you leave the Earth." She said.

I asked Sapphire, "I've been thinking about what you said about time meandering, circling. I don't understand how to think of non-linear time."

She hesitated a moment. She explored in my mind.

"That still tickles!" I said, clutching the back of my head.

"Thomas," she said, "this might be difficult for you, but let me try." She took a deep breath. "Time is like the wind."

"How's that?"

"Come to the cliff edge."

I followed her. "Look at the surface of the water." She said, "Tell me what you see."

"Well, it's pretty calm, mostly smooth, reflecting the sky light. There are darker patches where it's slightly ruffled by the wind."

"What is the direction of the wind?"

"There's a southerly, blowing straight up the river, about ten miles an hour."

"Describe the ruffles."

"Well, I've always been fascinated by them. It's beautiful the way they can persist and then change shape and move. There's a patch of rough in the middle of the river, upstream from the ferry crossing, towards Old Mill Creek. It's shaped like a kidney bean. Maybe a hundred yards long and fifty across."

"Please go on." She said.

"There's a smooth line, about four feet wide, winding east-west through the rough water. It's meandering like a woodland path. It's calm and still, with rough on either side. It stays in the same place."

"Go on."

"Now that path is slowly drifting downstream towards the south."

"Against the direction of the wind?"

"Yes."

"How can that be?"

"I don't know." I said.

"What you can see, Thomas, is the imprint of the wind on the water. Yes, it is moving overall from south to north, but it is not like a steam train moving over the land. It is more like the smoke from the train, like a cloud, tumbling in the air. Some gusts go up, some down, some spin, some eddy back on themselves. What you see on the water is like a handprint, hinting at the shape of the wind above it."

"The water moves in the same way. The tide might be coming in. The main current now runs fast upstream, but some water is almost still near the banks, some eddies in circles, some curls back against the tide.

"I see... I think."

"Time is like wind and the water. Time does not travel in straight lines. It circles and spirals. It moves organically. It meanders, eddies, wanders back and forth, up and down. It can progress in leaps. It can stand still in places while all about is in motion, like a woodland path through a stormy forest."

I just know I will be dreaming about the wind tonight.

Last night, I did dream about the wind. I was the wind. I was time. I was space and I was God. I moved upon the water, but randomly, without intention. I thundered around the world and burst across the Universe. I was supposed to be all-powerful, but I was being blown out of control wherever the wind would take me.

I woke with a burning question for Sapphire.

When we met I asked, "Forgive me, Sapphire if I tire you with my crude questions, but will you tell me more? Is there really a God?"

"Your questions will never tire me, Thomas, for you seek the truth and that is a noble aim."

"Like the God of Genesis?" I asked,

"You speak of the God of Earth, Thomas. That God was invented by you, the people of Earth, three to four thousand years ago, when you sought a meaning for life. Your elders wrote: *The Spirit moved upon the face of the waters and said, Let there be light, and there was light.*"

"That part was correct, Thomas. They were describing the One, which had existed forever, but then they added *'And God saw the light, that it was good: and God divided the light from the darkness.'* That's when your elders created a new idea, a judgemental God, a God of good and bad, right and wrong. A God of Ten Commandments, of rules, law and justice, a God of punishment and retribution. This was an angry God, a God of destruction."

"This was not the One, the God of Creation that made the Universe, the Earth, the sea, the whale, the tiger, the manitou, the buzzard, the robin, and the flea."

"The One is the creative energy and intelligence that

dreams the Universe. It is the One from which all life springs and which includes all life within it." She said. "The One has been for all time, billions of years and more. The One invented the Universe, all life and you."

"Will you tell me more about the One?" I asked.

"Thomas, the One is not something that can be told. It is not a story, a thing of words. It is something that can only be experienced. I have promised to take you to the One when you are ready. Please be patient."

9

Today Sapphire came to me and said, "Let us not talk of time, space, God and spirits, Thomas. Let us talk awhile about your life here, now, about your family, your granddaughter, for example."

"Willow?"

"Yes, do you like her name?"

"I thought it was a bit New Age, at first, but now I think it suits her."

"It should. We gave it to her."

"What? How? Er..." I bumbled.

Sapphire smiled. "Remember this?"

She took me back in memory, eleven years to Christmas, when Roland and Gemma were staying with us. Gemma was four months pregnant, and they knew it was a girl. Naomi was so excited.

We were talking about a name for the baby. Naomi suggested Chloe, Sophie, Freya. As usual, I made a joke of it and proposed Thomasina – after me, Elizabeth – after the Queen, Rooby – after the Labrador.

When Naomi called them for breakfast, the children came down all smiley and smug and said they'd decided on a name. They made Naomi and me guess for ten painful minutes and then said in unison.

"Her name is… roll of drums… Willow!"

Naomi asked, "When did you decide."

Gemma said, "It came to me in the night. The moon woke me up about three. I shook Rolly and said, 'I've got her name. It's Willow.' He snorted, rolled over and said, 'It's perfect.'"

After silently absorbing this little miracle, I asked Sapphire, "Why Willow?"

"We suggested Willow after a fine elegant and playful tree that loves to dance in the breeze.

"Well, that's her, always dancing." I said.

"But do not be fooled. Willow is the strongest tree in the forest. The wildest winds will tear an oak from the ground, but the willow is indestructible. Life will bend her, but it cannot break her."

"Our Willow can be pretty stubborn."

"More than that. The willow is immortal. She is not here

just once. Chop her down and she will grow back one hundred-fold. If just one willow twig breaks and falls to the moist soil, it will sprout into a whole new tree."

"Thomas, your grandchild was born on a special day for us, Mayday, and so she was born under the Sign of the Willow."

"I thought she was a Taurus. Stubborn as a bull." I said.

"I refer to the Celtic star signs: the Rowan, the Ash, Alder, Willow, Hawthorne, Oak, Holly, Hazel, Vine, Ivy, Reed, Elder, and the Birch. Your granddaughter was born on the first of May, which is between 15th April and 12th May, so, under the Sign of The Willow. Like the willow tree, she is ruled by the Moon. That is why she is so creative and intuitive. That is why she sparkles. Have you noticed she can see in the dark?"

"Can't say I have."

"The Moon gave her the Seeing. Remember, she could see me on her first visit to our village, yet it took you many days before you could see us. You had to drink from the spring. She did not need to."

"That's true."

"And from the Moon she knows that all life has its seasons. Everything, good or bad, will wax and wane like the Moon. Nothing is forever and she knows it. That is why she is so strong. She knows there will always be light after the dark. She knows every flower will die, and every storm will pass and both will come again."

I thought for a while and said, "How did you know her birthday? I don't think I've ever told you that?"

"We chose it."

"What?" My brain was pulsing like a jellyfish with all I had taken in.

"You remember when the children came to stay in the autumn before Gemma was with child."

"Yes, September first, just after Regatta."

"You remember they took a long walk, into the woods?"

"Yes, they were out most of the afternoon, into the evening."

"Well, Thomas, we were with them. We whispered them to a place that no other humans have been since we made our village here. It is a hard climb into the ravine below us from this side, but there is a hidden easy path from the other side of the valley. Deep in the ravine, a stream runs out to the river. There is an opening in the canopy where the sun reaches a grassy patch. A willow tree grows beside the stream. We whispered them to lie there and enjoy the sun for a while." She said.

"We lay my love and I, down by the weeping Willow." I said, "Is that when they conceived?"

"Yes."

"And nine months later…"

"Mayday!" She said, We also whispered blessings for the baby. We gave her the gift of Wonder, the love of Story, the gift of Song, the unfailing Memory of a Faerie and a sprinkle of our super senses."

"That explains a lot." I said, "May I bring her to see you? She would so love that."

"Of course, Thomas. I will send a friend to fetch you both."

This morning I had breakfast on the terrace with Naomi and Willow. Roland and Gemma had gone shopping across the river.

We watched the Navy cadets playing war games in the middle of the Dart. Two open launches circled a Motor Patrol Boat. The sailors on the launches had rifles. They exchanged blank rounds with those on the MPB.

Willow asked me, "Can I come with you to see the Faeries, Papa? Can I ask them some questions, like you do, Papa? Please can I?"

"It's strange you should say that, Willow, because only yesterday I asked Sapphire if you could visit her."

"What did she say, Papa?" Willow asked, eyes wide and fists tightly clenched.

"She said, she will send a friend to fetch us."

Willow screamed and danced a jig.

"Willow," I said, "I think you should ask your Grandma first."

"OK." She said and ran off to see Naomi, who was in the kitchen.

When she returned she said, "Grandma said I can go, so long as I am very careful not to make any promises to them and to tell her everything that happens."

I said, "That's wonderful, but Willow, before we go, you must promise not to get excited and frighten her away. You must be still and quiet."

"I will. I promise." She said.

"OK, let's go."

Willow grabbed my hand and dragged me along. She stoped to ask Joe's Faerie the way and Willow's dove took off from the Faerie's head and flew ahead.

As we reached the top of the stone steps. Willow stopped, turned to me, finger on lips. The dove was perched on a branch *Coo Cooing*. There was a faint rustling in the undergrowth below. I could see a smudge of rusty red. A solitary roe deer lifted her head. She stared at us for a moment. Big black eyes. Her ears twitched. She barked, B*ouffff-bouff-bouff*, turned and loped away, her white rump bobbing into the shadows. "It's Bambi Papa! The Faeries sent Bambi!"

The dove flew high into the trees.

When we arrived at the Glen, I dropped into my chair and Willow sat beside me. Sapphire appeared and hovered before us.

Anticipating Willow's reaction, I placed one hand firmly on her shoulder. She took the hint and sat silently, though quivering with excitement.

Sapphire said. "Welcome, Willow. We are so happy to see you again. We thank you for bringing your grandfather to us.

He has become a good friend. We hope you will be our friend too."

"Oh! That's wonderful!" Willow shouted, "I would love to be your friend!" She made to stand, poised to run towards Sapphire.

I squeezed her shoulder, reminding her to be still.

"Will you teach me about Faeries?" Willow asked.

"Of course Willow. Would you like to ask a question?"

"Yes. Please. Can I ask anything?"

"Of course, whatever you want to know." Sapphire said.

Oh no! I thought. I remembered the first time Willow asked Naomi the same question.

Willow was seven. Roland and Gemma brought her to stay. We all sat round the fire one evening having tea and cake.

Willow said, "Grandma, Can I ask you a Question."

Naomi said, "Of course, you can ask anything, me darlin' girl."

"Well, when did you and Papa have your first kiss?"

Roland and Gemma looked shocked.

"Oh my!" I said, "Willow that's a bit personal."

"No, Tom. She's just curious." Naomi said, "Why shouldn't she know. I'll tell you, Willow. It was in the very first second that we met!"

"No!" Willow sucked in a deep breath. Her eyes widened.

"It was 1945 on V.E.Day in Bristol. Everyone was out on the streets, thousands of us, celebrating the end of the war. We were all so happy. We were a-dancing and a-drinking with our friends and hugging and kissing. I turned round and saw this handsome young soldier drinking up a storm with his pals. I looked at him. He looked at me. He turned away from his mates and came running over and gave me the biggest hug and the sweetest kiss right on the lips."

"Oh Grandma! That's wonderful!"

"He asked for my name. I said, 'I'm Naomi but friends call me Nay.' He said, 'I'm Thomas.' I asked him, 'What shall I call you?' He said 'Thomas, Tommy, Tom, whatever you like.' I said, 'OK, Thomas, Tommy, Tom-Tom, come and join our party.'"

"From that moment we never left each other. I took him home. I told Mother, 'He's called Thomas, Tommy, Tom-Tom and he's fresh off the ship.' When Father heard Tom had nowhere to stay, he insisted he should lodge with us."

Willow said, "Grandma, did you fall in love?"

"Willow!" I protested.

Naomi said, "Never mind your Grandpa! Yes we did, Willow, right from the start, but neither of us let on straight away. He was so easy to tease. When we sat round the dinner table, Mother put him right next to me."

"Oh I remember it so well. You know he whispered to me 'Are you all Irish?' I put on the accent and said, 'Ah, b'gorrah, to be sure, to be sure. County Cork born and bred. Now, where are you from, Englishman?'"

"Thomas Tommy Tom-Tom put on an even thicker accent and said, 'Oooh Arrh, I be a Devon boy! Son of the soil.' I said 'What do you do, my pretty Devon Boy?' He said, 'I make things for purty folk like you, m'Lady. Things like chairs, tables and sideboards and such. I work wi' me 'ands.'"

"I said, 'Well, Mary, Joseph 'n Jesus, would you believe it, so do I, Thomas, Tommy, Tom-Tom. I play a mean fiddle and paint pictures nice people buy. I think we'll get along mighty well.'"

"And we did, Willow. We fell in love and we got married and we never fell out of love." Naomi looked to me with a gentle, sad smile. "Even though we've been though the hardest of times, Willow, we are still, and always will be, the very best of friends."

Willow looked from Sapphire to me, as if for permission for the question that was bubbling on her lips, but before I could respond she blurted, "Do you have a toilet?"

"Willow!" I looked to Sapphire and raised my hands in apology.

"A very good question," Sapphire said, smiling "for the answer will teach you much about Faeries."

I couldn't wait to hear.

"We do not need toilets. If we drink too much water, it evaporates from our wings, so we don't need to pee."

Willow covered her mouth to stifle a giggle. She'd never heard a Faerie say "Pee."

"We eat very little and we burn it all into energy, so there's no waste, so we don't need to poop."

"That's amazing!" Willow said, "Can I ask some more?"

"Ask all day and all night, my beautiful child." Sapphire said.

"What do you eat?"

"We don't need to eat much. We get most of our energy directly from sunlight and moonlight falling on our wings. We nibble certain plants and flowers to keep our bodies healthy." Sapphire said.

"You're a vegetable!" Willow laughed.

Sapphire looked to me, puzzled.

I shrugged.

"You're a vegetable, like me. Daddy says 'You are what you eat.' I eat vegetables so I must be a vegetable and so are you!"

Willow giggled, Sapphire joined in, clapped her hands and danced a pirouette. Willow did the same..

I was delighted they were getting on so well.

"How do you sleep?" Willow asked.

"We sleep in gossamer hammocks."

"Don't your wings stick out?"

"We fold our wings and curl up on our sides."

"I do that." Willow said. "How do you wash your clothes?"

"We have no need. You never see a butterfly washing its wings, or a badger combing its hair."

Willow laughed.

"The wind and the rain keep us clean and sometimes we play in the stream."

"Willow," I said, "these are very personal questions!"

"'Tis no matter, Thomas." Sapphire said, "Children ask the very best questions. Go on, Willow. What else can we tell you?"

"OK. Where are your babies?"

"We have no babies."

"Well, how do make new fairies?"

"We call it the Doubling."

"What's that?"

"We copy ourselves. One faerie can become two. It only takes a few seconds.'

Willow said, "I'd love to see that!"

Sapphire said, "There is not much to see. One Faerie sings and vibrates into a blur and then when she stops vibrating, there are two."

Willow thought for awhile.

"What if you die? Can you die?"

"This body I live in can die. My body was trodden-on once by a cow. That was not pleasant. But then one of my sisters Doubled me into a new body.

Willow thought again and said, "So, no children? No parents?"

"That's right Willow, We are all the same, like sisters."

"I don't have a sister." Willow said.

"You are *my* sister." Sapphire said.

Willow stood with her mouth wide open, not knowing what this meant or how to respond. She looked back to me, her face a question – *Really?* I smiled and nodded. She sighed deeply.

"What else do you wish to know?" Sapphire asked.

"Do you go to Faerie school?"

"We do not need school. Whatever one Faerie learns is shared instantly with every Faerie in the world. We all learn for each other."

"No schools. No lessons. No exams?" Willow said.

"None of that." Sapphire said.

Willow said, "Do you like making up stories? I do."

"All the time. We are as old as the mountains. We have seen much happen. We tell stories about what we have seen."

"Mmm. Can you do magic?"

"What we do might look like magic to you, but think about this carefully, Willow. It is just that we can do things in the world that you cannot do yet. That is what you call magic."

"Tell me some Faerie magic."

"If you see a Faerie appear out of nowhere and then disappear instantly, you might think it is like a magician's disappearing trick. But we would just be stepping into another time or another dimension that you cannot see. No magic. No trick, just something you do not yet understand."

Willow sat in silence for a moment, and Sapphire and I kept quiet while she churned over what she'd heard.

Willow's dove flew down from the canopy and rested on a lower branch nearby. Willow suddenly jumped up and flapped her arms and said, "Can you teach me to fly?"

"You cannot fly with the body you live in, Willow, but you can fly without it. Would you like to fly with me?"

"Oh yes! Can we? Can we please, Papa?"

I nodded enthusiastically.

Sapphire said, "Where would you like to go? Somewhere really exciting? Like, Alpha Centauri, the Moon, India, Japan?"

"Can we go see the county fair?"

"Lie down on the grass." Sapphire said, "Both of you. Close your eyes. Breathe slowly and deeply. Count back in your head from one hundred."

"A hundred, ninety-nine, ninety-eight, ninety ..."

"Not aloud, Willow. In your head."

I counted with Willow. Soon I was floating. Willow rose into the air. I saw our sleeping bodies. Then we flew with Sapphire, above the woods and over fields and lanes and roads, going faster and faster. Soon we were hovering over a big showground outside the city of Exeter. We flew low and could see the prize-winning cows with rosettes round their necks, the sheepdogs herding their little flocks. We could hear the shepherd's calls and whistles. We could see lines of shiny new yellow tractors. From the fairground, we heard the deep-base of pop music and the screams of kids on the rides. We flew slowly back to Quay Cottage and hovered over our bodies, drifted back inside and opened our eyes.

Willow leapt up and danced wildly. "That was wonderful, Papa. Can we do it again?"

Sapphire said, "You can do it whenever you wish, Willow, but it will be harder by yourself. You will need to practice. It will be easier when you are dreaming."

"But I'm asleep when I'm dreaming. So, how could I?" Willow asked.

"Sometimes you might be dreaming and realise for a second that you are in a dream. When that happens, just jump up into the sky, and you will be able to fly. Perhaps just a little at first, but with practice you will be able to fly anywhere."

Willow looked at me. "Wow!" She said.

I said, "Maybe that's enough questions for one day. Sapphire, may we return tomorrow?"

"You will be most welcome."

Willow ran in to see Naomi.
"Had fun in the woods?" Naomi asked.
"We've been to the county fair, Grandma. We flew there!"
"Your Grandpa Tom tells great stories."
"No, Grandma, we really…"
"Help me peel some spuds."

On our way back to the woods, I asked Willow if she could keep her questions a little less personal this time.

"OK, Papa." She said, cheerfully.

As soon as she saw Sapphire, Willow asked, "Can I ask some more questions?"

"Of course Willow. Ask whatever you want."

"Well, you know yesterday you said you don't have to make Faerie babies? I've been thinking about that."

I shot Willow a warning glance.

Sapphire said, "Yes?"

"*Oh no!*" I thought.

Willow said, "Well… Does that mean… you have no…?"

"Willow!" I protested.

"That's right, Willow," Sapphire said, "No reproductive organs."

I shook my head at Willow and gave Sapphire an apologetic look. She smiled.

Willow frowned deeply, trying to absorb this intimate revelation. "So, are you like…"

Sapphire and I watched her struggling.

"Like a Barbie Doll." I whispered.

"Oh… I see." Willow said.

"And, since I'm sure it will answer you next question, we have no mammary glands." Sapphire said.

Willow looked deep I thought for a while. She said, "Ohhhhh."

Then she asked Sapphire, "Are you the same as the Angels?"

"Oh no." Sapphire said, "They are more powerful than Faerie Folk. They bring spirits into the world and take them out. Faeries cannot do that."

"So what's your job then?"

"Our job is to keep a close watch over humans. We are here to add a little joy to your lives and to reduce, the sickness and weeping in the world.

"How do you do that?"

"Many ways, Willow. We hang dewdrops on spider webs, so you will enjoy the early morning. In Winter, we work with Jack Frost to paint your windows, so you look forward to the cold. We plant the bluebells to invite you to come walk in the woods."

"I love Bluebells." Willow said, "But Grandma says you mustn't pick them, or they'll miss their sisters, get lonely and sad and die in a day."

"Not always," Sapphire said, and flew high into the oak. She returned with an armful of bluebells and handed them to Willow.

"Take this gift, to your grandmother, Willow. Death is not always forever."

"I will." Willow said, "Do you make the weather?"

"Not the big things like storms and floods. That's the work of the Spirits of Wind and Water. We can play with the wind and make dust devils or make quick rain showers. We can make shapes in the clouds – people and animals, so when you look up you remember you are a small part of a big planet. We sing the rainbows to give you something to look forward to after the rain."

Willow sang: "I can sing a rainbow. Sing a rainbow. Sing a rainbow, too."

"But our real work here is to reduce human suffering – to heal you, body and soul."

"You made Papa Tom better." Willow said, "You gave him honey."

"Yes, and we make potions from the plants of the forest to heal people. At night, when humans are sleeping, we fly out and visit the poorly ones. We can tell what ails them, and we give them medicine."

"Do you wake them up?"

"No, we drop the potions into their ears or mouths."

"When they snore!" Willow laughed.

Sapphire smiled.

Willow's dove flew down from the oak and rested on the arm of my chair. Willow reached into her pocket for some seed mix. The dove hopped to her wrist and pecked the seed from her hand. Willow cradled the dove in her arms and stroked her wings.

"Do you look after animals?" She asked, "Like birds, like doves?"

"We do, Willow, especially this one." Sapphire pointed at the white dove and glanced at me.

Willow looked pensive for a moment.

"None of my friends at school have ever seen a Faerie." She said.

"We rarely show ourselves to humans. But occasionally we need their help, or they need our help."

"Why did you come to me, that day. Why me?" Willow frowned deeply.

"Long ago, one like you, with the flaming hair, helped us, and we promised to help her family in their time of need. We came to you first, Willow, for you had the Seeing. Then you invited your grandfather, and he invited your grandmother."

"Grandma doesn't want to see you." Willow said.

"She will, in time. She knows we are here to help her and your grandfather. They have both suffered more than their share of weeping."

Willow looked at me with concern. I smiled. She turned

back to Sapphire and asked, "What's the Seeing?"

"The Seeing and the Hearing are gifts the Moon gave you when you were born. They help you see and hear Faeries and other creatures. We Faeries other gifts – the Love of Life, the Love of Story, Dance and Song and the Love of Nature. We also gave you unfailing Memory."

"Well I do love to dance and sing and Daddy says I have the memory of an elephant."

"Your father is right to say that. Elephants remember everything that any elephant has ever learned since their species was created in the world. It is like the memory of a Faerie. We remember everything we learned back down all the ages, to the Dreamtime, when your world was sung into being."

"What can I give back, to thank you for your gifts to me?" Willow asked.

"All we wish, Willow, is that you use your gifts to bring more joy into the world."

"I'll do that!" Willow said.

When we returned home, I said, "Just go see Grandma, and tell her what happened."

When Willow returned, she said, "I told her everything. I gave her the Faerie bluebells. First, she didn't want them, she said, 'I never have flowers in the house 'cos I don't like watching things die.' I said, 'You should never refuse a Faerie gift.' and she said, 'You should never accept one.' I said, 'You can say goodnight to them at bedtime, and they'll say good morning.' She said 'Oh, all right then.' I put them in a jar by her bed."

"Oh, I forgot, Grandma said she has a few questions to

ask the Faeries."

"Perhaps she'll come with us tomorrow." I said.

I asked Naomi if she would like to come meet the Faeries with us today, but she refused. So, Willow and I climbed the hill together.

Sapphire asked, "Thomas, Willow, my lovely friends, what questions do you have today?"

Willow leapt in. "I have a question. When Papa met you, he was very sick. How did you make him better."

"Would you like to see our pharmacy, where we prepare our remedies?" Sapphire asked.

"That would be marvellous."

"Both of you, lie on the grass." Sapphire said, "You know what to do. Close your eyes."

We were flying again with Sapphire.

"Follow me." She said, and we flew into an opening in the oak tree, up through a long vertical tube and out high in the open canopy, out of sight and reach of prying humans and hungry deer and rabbits.

Willow cried, "Look Papa!"

We saw a fabulous garden. It spread along the branches and up the trunk. Hundreds of plants grew in wide gossamer glass channels spread along the boughs and spiralling up the trunk.

Sapphire spread her arms and said "Welcome to our Sky Garden."

I said, "This is huge. Why couldn't we see it from the ground."

"Remember I told you, Thomas, we can make transparent gossamer glass that has no reflections."

"Invisible glass!" Willow said.

A score of Faeries flitted around tending the plants. In this fabulous garden they grew every herb, plant, lichen, and fungus you could imagine and many more which you could not.

"This is one of the things we do for you. Here's how we made your honey drops. Watch." Sapphire said.

She flew among the plants, picking a stem here and there as she sang their names.

"Muckruth Root, Devil Berries, Blister Cress, Viper Spit, Gagliafrasse, Docklaurel, Shimmer Nut Oil, Thunderseed, Blood Anise, Cavern Rue, Common Hazel Moss and here's the Stinky Mallow."

"They sound familiar." I said.

"Yes, Thomas, they are in your prescription, remember? These plants are part of you. Their essences and their spirits entered your body through your honey. Come, let me show you how we prepare them."

She flew into an opening in the trunk carrying her bunch of plants.

"Welcome to the Pharmacy." She said.

"Whoa!" Willow said, eyes wide.

The gigantic chamber was almost entirely filled from floor to ceiling and wall to wall with gossamer glass shelves suspended on fine gossamer rope ladders. The shelves to our left were crammed with plant specimens in gossamer jars, some still growing with their stems in water. Some plants were hung in bunches upside down, drying out. Hundreds of jars were filled with mosses, lichens, and fungi. Behind these were more shelves with jars of seeds.

On the far side of the chamber, a gossamer glass slab ran

the length of the curved wall. Faeries worked with an intricate construction of glass cauldrons, flasks and jars, connected by spiralling glass tubes. Sapphire fed each of her chosen plants into individual glass hoppers, from which each plant followed its own path through the complex of tubes and flasks.

Some were sliced, some diced, some ground into powder. Some fell into cauldrons of clear liquid and dissolved. Others were distilled and collected in condensing flasks. Finally they were injected into tiny honey-filled glass phials.

Sapphire said, "This is how the plant the essences go into your honey."

I asked, "It looks like each plant gets its own treatment. How can that be?"

"Just listen." Sapphire said.

Willow said, "All the Faeries are singing different tunes."

Sapphire said, "Each plant is guided by it's own tune." She smiled and flew us back to the clearing.

Willow said, "I have to go now. We're going back to London. Can I come see you again?"

"That will be wonderful." Sapphire said.

Willow told Naomi, "Grandma, we saw them making medicines!"

"Oh, really? Did they wave a wand and magic them from fresh air?"

"No, Grandma, they have a huge invisible Sky Garden where they grow everything. They collect the flowers and put them in a glass machine, and they sing to them into medicines. It's amazing!"

"Sweet girl. You have such a vivid imagination."

"How are the Faerie bluebells?" Willow asked.

"Oh, they're dead already. I must throw them out. Want to come shopping with me before you go home?"

"Can I drive the trolley?"

"Come on then. Go get Roo."

10

When Willow and Naomi returned from shopping, we waved the family off, and I came up to see Sapphire on my own. When we met, she said, "Willow is a beautiful creature."

"That she is." I said. I hesitated and took a deep breath. "Sapphire, yesterday, you told Willow that Naomi and I had suffered more than our share of weeping. What did you mean?"

"I was thinking about your Lost One."

"Oh!" I said, "I didn't think you would know about that. I haven't thought about her for a long time."

I dropped into my chair.

"You never stop thinking about her, Thomas, she is always in the front of your mind, where I cannot help seeing it. She is the real reason for your sadness, not the loss of youth and health."

"You're right, Sapphire."

"Do you want to talk about her."

"Not really. It was a long time ago, decades."

"But it feels like yesterday?"

"Yes. It does." I admitted.

"Will you tell me, Thomas?"

"You could just tickle my memories and find out for yourself."

"I do not wish to do that. Please tell what you wish to tell, in your own time, in your own way."

I hesitated again. I wanted to avoid stirring up the old pain. We were silent for some time.

I said, "Roland was a lovely baby, laughing, cooing, curious, wide awake, eyes everywhere. We both loved him. Then Naomi wanted to try for a little girl."

"When she fell pregnant, she was delighted. We both were. When they told us it was a girl, well, that was one of the happiest days of our lives. Naomi threw a party and invited friends, neighbours and the family on both sides. It was such a happy time for us. We had a Name the Baby contest and the most popular choice was Daisy, and we added Lee for Naomi's father."

"And then?"

"The pregnancy seemed to go well, but the twelve-week tests showed something wrong with Daisy. They did more tests, eight weeks later, and told us little Daisy was suffering from a rare condition, which meant she would have misformed organs and would probably die before the birth. They said, if she did live, it would be for a short time, and she would suffer from heart defects, lung, kidney, and stomach problems."

"It was a terrible blow to both of us, but Naomi was determined to have the baby. I was frightened for the child and for what it would do to Naomi if the baby died before birth or lived a life of pain."

"The doctor said we should think about a termination. To me, this seemed the best way. I tried to convince Naomi to have an abortion, but she was shocked that I'd even consider such a thing. She was adamant. She said, 'Our little girl deserves a life. I can look after her, whatever might be wrong with her. Will you pray with me, Thomas?'"

"I said, 'You know I'm not a great believer.'"

"'Daisy Lee needs all our prayers.' She said. We held hands and closed our eyes."

"Naomi said, 'Please God, save our little Daisy Lee.' I repeated, 'Please God, save our little Daisy Lee'"

"But," Sapphire asked, "is that all you prayed for?"

"I must go now." I said, and I left for the cottage.

As I approached the terrace, I saw a scrap of paper on the table. It was yellow vellum, the same as in the Journal. A note was written in Sapphire's elegant script:

"He who learns must suffer. And even in our sleep, pain that cannot forget falls drop by drop upon the heart, and in our own despair, against our will, comes wisdom to us by the awful grace of God." — Aeschylus"

I returned to Sapphire, hoping she would show me some more amazing Faerie technologies, but as soon as she appeared she said, "'Please God, save our little Daisy Lee.' Was there more, Thomas?"

She smiled.

I hesitated.

She smiled.

"Well, yes." I said, reluctantly.

"Do you wish to tell me?"

"Well, I did say the prayer aloud; 'Please God, save our little Daisy Lee.' and then, in my head, I continued my prayer, '... from a life of pain and sorrow. Please, God, take Daisy back to Heaven and bring Naomi another healthy child.'"

I sat with my head in my hands. My eyes washed with tears.

Sapphire said. "Thank you, Thomas. I appreciate your courage and honesty."

I sobbed, "I hoped that Naomi would change her mind and let the doctors terminate, or, if not, that God would take little Daisy naturally before her birth. I cried next to Naomi in the dark, night after night. I felt so ashamed. How could a father want an innocent child to die?"

"I know." Sapphire said.

"Daisy was born full term on 1st May 1947. That's a day I'll never forget. I held Naomi's hand and breathed in time with her, encouraging her to push. At the same time, I was praying for a stillbirth!"

I waited for my tears to pass.

"If the Devil had come at that time and told me he had a place in hell for me, I would have followed him meekly."

"When the baby emerged, the nurses scooped her up and turned away from us. We heard a slap. Daisy Lee took her first breath and squealed. This was not the cry of a newborn bursting into the world and filling her lungs, like a diver coming up for air. It was a feeble whimper of pain. I could see her tiny clenched-up body contorting. She was fighting for her life. Naomi realised it was bad, and she screamed, 'Save my baby! Save my baby!'"

"I prayed again that God would take Daisy right now and

put an end to her agony, but her torture continued. Naomi sat upright, held out her arms, and screamed, 'Give me my baby!' When Naomi saw the child, she drew back and cried out. Her first reaction was shock, but that quickly turned to compassion. She cradled the baby in her arms. She held her swollen head in her hand and stroked her scrunched up little face. Naomi rocked her baby. She watched helplessly as her baby struggled for every breath. Little Daisy coughed and was still. It was over."

"One nurse took the baby. The other glanced at the wall clock. She made a note. Daisy had lived for ten minutes."

"I fell into the visitor's chair and silently thanked God for the end to Daisy's torture. Naomi must have taken my expression for relief. She turned to me and screamed like a witch in a fire, 'You! You! You wanted an abortion. You wanted her dead! It was you, Thomas Archer, you wicked, wicked man!'"

"I could say nothing. She screamed and pulled at her hair. 'You put a curse on my baby, Thomas Archer. I curse you from the bottom of my heart. I curse you forever.'"

"I tried to put my arms around her, but she beat my chest and clawed at me. When all her energy was spent, she fell into deep sobs and buried her head in the pillows. The Doctor gave her a sedative. She said, 'You need to leave, Mr. Archer. Let her rest.'"

Sapphire asked, "And later?"

"We took the taxi home from the hospital in silence. Naomi wouldn't look at me. There was silence in the house for weeks. If I tried to talk, she'd turn away."

"When she did finally talk, it was just for management.

'Tea's ready.' or 'I'm off to bed.' I didn't push her. I didn't want to say anything that would fire up her distress."

"In time she softened. We made polite conversation, we got on with our mostly separate lives. We lived like house mates. To outsiders, we looked like a normal happy couple. But under the surface, Naomi was full of blame, and I was full of guilt."

Sapphire asked, "How did Naomi learn of your silent prayer?"

"One evening we were sitting on the terrace, quietly watching the river. Naomi kept glowering at me, then quickly lowering her gaze. Her face was pink. She looked like a volcano about to erupt. Then she said, in a controlled, flat voice: 'We both prayed for her, Tom. Why didn't God listen to us?' She looked straight into my eyes."

"I hesitated, scared to speak, frightened of her response. I took a deep breath and blurted out the confession that had been bursting to escape my lips. 'He did listen, Nay. That time when we prayed. I asked God to save our Daisy Lee and then, I asked him to take her back to heaven and bring...'"

"Naomi's face reddened. She shouted, 'What! You prayed for our little girl to die?' She held her hands to her face and she screamed, 'What did you ask Him to do?'"

"I said, 'Nay, I am so sorry. I prayed for her to be still born. Then, when she lived and howled in pain, I asked God to take her away quickly and to...'"

"But she didn't let me finish. She screamed, 'What kind of father wants an abortion, and when he doesn't get one, he prays twice more for his child to die! What kind of monster are you?'"

"I tried to finish: 'But I...'"

"She stopped me. She screamed: 'You killed my baby! Three times!' I couldn't look at her."

"Sapphire, I've gone over this every night before sleep and again in my dreams. I told Naomi, 'I thought it was for the best! I am so sorry!' She said, 'You're Sorry? Well, now you can ask God to take me, because I don't want to live any more without my baby. I can't live with a wicked man like you. You're sorry? Sorry? I will pray to the Devil that he takes you back – to hell!'"

"She grabbed her handbag and ran from the house, slamming the door behind her. She scooped up Roland who was playing in the yard and dragged him to the ferry, which was about to leave. I looked to the ferry and saw her clutching Roland tightly to her chest, staring at me with hatred in her eyes."

"I didn't see her for a week. She must have stayed with friends across the river. When she came back, she walked in, didn't look at me, settled Roland down and went to the kitchen. She said, with her back to me, 'I expect you're hungry.'"

"It was a terrible time for both of us. In the months that followed I pleaded with her, many times, 'Nay, we could try again and maybe God will bring Daisy back to us.' But each time I mentioned it, she sank into deep, silent depression that could last for weeks."

"That was your time of much weeping." Sapphire said.

"Yes, and it didn't stop there. Every day, for years, she's had to say Daisy's name out loud. Each morning she counts the sugar lumps into the tea she says, 'One for you. One for me. One for little Daisy Lee.' Sometimes she stares at me, as if to say, 'I remember what you did.'"

Sapphire asked, "How did you survive your sadness?"

"We got on with our lives. Roland was just a toddler, very active and demanding. Naomi poured her love into him. Her mother, Eleanor, got sick and slowly began to forget the world. Naomi cared for her until the world let her go. Naomi became the hub of her family and held her brothers and sisters together. The nephews and nieces all loved their Auntie Nay."

"She had her local arty friends. She loved her cooking, painting, and music. She'd often close herself away in the greenhouse and play Irish tunes on her fiddle for hours."

"I threw myself into work, making fine furniture for wealthy people."

Despite everything, we were still friends. I still loved her. I cared for her and I know despite everything she cared for me. We had a good enough life. We treated each other gently, but we didn't touch. She seldom took my hand, never accepted a hug. We slept apart, of course."

"Her blame and my guilt were still bubbling below and would sometimes erupt. Naomi once asked if I would come to church for an Easter service. I said, 'I'd rather not, I'm not feeling so good.' She said, 'No! You're not feeling good about going to church, are you! That's because, you can't forgive God for taking Daisy away! And you can't forgive yourself for begging him to do it three times! And nor can I!'"

"She was right, Sapphire," I said, "I had wished for our child to die."

"But you wished it out of love for your child and your wife, and you wished for a new child to take Daisy's place."

"I tried many times to tell her that, but she'd have none of it. She'd say, 'It's no good lying now, Tom. You know you asked God to kill our child.'"

"I waited for her to get over the loss. I waited one year, then another. In time, I stopped waiting. We put our loss behind us."

"And Willow?" Sapphire asked.

"When Willow was born, Naomi threw all her love into her and so did I. She has brought joy into our lives again. But often I see Naomi looking at Willow with tears in her eyes, mourning our lost girl."

"Sapphire," I said, my eyes brimming with tears, "I wish I could go back to that maternity room and pray simply for Daisy to live."

"Thomas, You did pray for Daisy's spirit to live. I know because I was there."

"You were there?"

"We Faerie Folk were there, ready to bless the baby. We heard your prayers, all of them. So did the Angels. So did your God."

"But Naomi didn't hear it all." I said.

"Perhaps it is time she did." Sapphire said, "Will you invite her again to meet with us?"

That evening, I asked Naomi if she would come to see the Faeries, but she refused. "I've too much to do here to go gallivanting in the woods with Fae Folk."

11

Last night, a northerly storm raged down the river. In the morning, coated, hooded and Wellington-booted, I struggled up the cliff. The wind was gusting strong enough to swipe me off my feet. Rain and mud cascaded over the screes, making it hard to secure each step. When I reached the Glen, the rain had funnelled down between the hills. A torrent about three feet wide and two feet deep rushed towards the opening of the Faerie village. The deluge hit the huge oak boughs at the entrance at about forty-five degrees and then ran alongside.

Where the boughs lay on top of each other, they diverted the flood well, but where the water and mud reached the gap between the tree-giant's crossed fingers, it spilled over and thundered through. It gouged out the Faerie's pure water stream, carved a trench for a few feet, burst over the edge and cascaded into the ravine.

I didn't see the Faeries. They were sheltering inside the tree, but I heard Sapphire's voice in my head, over the roar of the storm.

"We cannot fly in this tempest. The wind and rain will destroy us.

We cannot escape underground, the tunnels are flooded. We are trapped inside the oak. Our village is in grave danger, Thomas. There is a waterfall eroding the cliff edge. Mud and rocks are falling over and carving the channel wider and deeper. It could undermine the roots of the oak if it spreads further."

"And the wind is trying to tip the oak toward the cliff edge." I thought.

"What can we do?"

"I'll be back soon."

I scrambled down to the house. I ran to my workshop and gathered a sheet of tarpaulin. I rolled it up and tied a loop of rope at each end and made a shoulder strap between the loops. I flung it over my head and chest and grabbed a hammer. I emptied a box of galvanised roof nails into my coat pocket. I climbed back to the Glen, a muddy, slippery trip with my awkward load.

I waded into the storm torrent. The current was strong and threatened to sweep me off my feet. I struggled to the gap in the boughs. I unfolded the tarp bit by bit and hammered roof nails into the upper bough to secure it. I battled with the wind, which violently inflated the tarp like a sail and tried to wrest it from my hands.

I jammed a boot under the lowest bough, but the force of the deluge tore it loose. I lost my footing. I held on to the tarp. I was being dragged towards the cliff edge. I was terrified. I thought this was my last moment on Earth, but the roof nails held the tarp. I clung on and climbed astride the top bough, out of the water for a while.

When I'd nailed the top of the tarp securely, I slipped back into the water. I unrolled the upstream corner of the tarp, held it down to the submerged lower bough and hammered it in. I was hammering under the muddy torrent, with my head above water, but my body and hands below. I couldn't see the hammer or the nail. I hit my frozen fingers more than the nails. The current tried to tear the tarp from my hand. Once the first nail was in and the corner of the tarp was secure, I hit nails along the entire upstream edge.

I slowly worked my way along and nailed the lower edge of the tarp to the lower bough. My whole body was now drenched and frozen as the flood, blocked from its escape through the gap, hit me with full force. At last, the gap was covered, and it diverted the water along the boughs. The stream widened and dissipated harmlessly over the sloping clearing.

I drove in more nails where I thought the water might work its way through, and finally, I climbed out of the deluge and up to the bank. I lay there, curled in a foetal position, shivering violently.

In my head, I heard a chorus of cheers and whoops from the Faeries in the tree, but I was too exhausted to celebrate. I rolled to my knees, painfully stood, and made my slow way down the cliff to home.

The following day there was not a breath of wind, a clear blue sky and not a single cloud. The river ran red with the iron-rich soil eroded from the upstream woods and farms, and was scattered with torn branches and twigs.

When I arrived at the Glen, a swarm of Faeries flew out and danced before me. They sang a beautiful song in complex harmony. I could make out some words, about the birth signs of the trees and the special qualities they bestowed, upon those born under their influence.

Their song ended. They flew back into the village, leaving Sapphire, who hovered before me.

"Our song is to show our deep gratitude for your protection." She said, "You saved our village from the storm. We will be forever grateful to you."

"It's what I promised I would do."

"Today, Thomas, we sang two things of great importance. We sung a trench across the stream's path well above the village. If there is another storm, it will divert the surge over the cliff edge well before it threatens us."

"I am very pleased to hear that." I said.

"And we sung this for you, a small gift."

A party of ten Faeries flew from the fallen boughs and placed something on the grass before me — an exquisite golden bowl.

"Please take it." Sapphire said.

It was like the one I'd seen the Faeries working. It was fringed with tiny Faerie figures in the treetops. In the centre of the base, was an elderly human face, a little like mine.

"We sang it to make a memory of the storm and how you turned the deluge away. Please accept our gift and take it to your home."

"It is charming. Thank you."

When I presented the bowl to Naomi, I said, "It's from the Faeries, to thank me for saving their Village from the storm."

"Well, it's lovely, Tom. Put it there."

I placed it in the nook in the kitchen wall, along with our charity shop treasures.

"Oh, that reminds me." I said, "How are your Bluebells coming on?"

"We'll, they wilted after just a day. I meant to throw them out, but I forgot. Next day they came back all perky. Never seen anything like it. It's been weeks now. Pretty things, they are."

I have come to think that my life has become full of surprises and discoveries, some welcome, some challenging. I've just received a surprise email from an ex-girlfriend of Young Nathan, Naomi's nephew, the son of her brother, William.

I'll tell you what's in the message, which I think you will find interesting, but first I need to give a little background.

Naomi's relations have a habit of turning up uninvited. Last Friday, we had a surprise visit from Nathan.

I was home alone. Naomi, was on the other side, shopping, having a proper coffee at the Inn on Bayard's Cove, catching up with friends.

I hadn't seen Nathan for a couple of years, but I remember him as a chip off the old block, big voice, big feet, self-serving, a charmer. He's seventeen now.

He knocked loudly at the front door.

"Hello, Nathan, what a nice surprise!" I said, "We don't see you very often!"

"Well, I had to see my favourite Uncle Tom." He boomed.

He stepped in without invitation.

"And when we do see you," I continued, "it's when you want something from us. How can we help you this time?"

"Well," he said, in a voice, too bass for his years. "You know I have this eczema..." He held up his right arm, red with blotches. Mum and Dad are fed up buying me Cortisone ointments. So, they've agreed to pay for this new experimental treatment for me at the Nuffield in Plymouth. Oh, this is Suze." He waved his arm at something behind him.

I couldn't see Suze, just a mop of brown hair that hung over a person's face. Only her nose was visible. I smiled. She recoiled like I'd done something obscene and sloped into the room.

Now I could see, her whole person was hung like her hair. The brown hoodie, which she must have stolen from a Hobbit, hung from her slight shoulders. It completely covered her body like a curtain, all the way down to her well-scuffed Doc Marten's.

"Nice to meet you." I said, offering my hand.

She stepped away, gave me a sneering "Whatever!", sidled out to the terrace and sat with her bored face in her skinny hands, watching the river.

"So, that's where we're going, Plymouth." Nathan said, waving a newspaper cutting about the hospital. "Treatment takes 48 hours, so I need to stay for three nights. I thought I'd ask Suze along to make a trip of it. Only thing is... I had my card stolen yesterday."

This story already sounded too complex to be true.

"Oh, dear! That's such bad luck!" I said.

"Yea. In the pub. No problem, though. They're sending a new one."

"That's all right, then?" I said.

"Yeah, but I won't get it until I get home."

"Of course."

"So, I find myself embarrassed in the cashflow department."

"I see." I said, "Can't your parents help?"

"They're on holiday in Florence."

"That's inconvenient."

"So, as we were driving nearby, I thought I'd drop in to Dartmouth, pop across on the ferry and see if my favourite Uncle Tom could kindly sub me some cash to get through the trip?"

"I see. How much do you need?"

He looked up to his forehead, consulting his shopping list.

"Well there's petrol, the hotel, food, and drink. Can you spare about three hundred?"

I took a deep breath. "Sorry, Nathan, we don't have that sort of money in the house."

"We could ferry you across to the cashpoint in Dartmouth."

"How very thoughtful of you, Nathan, but that's a whole month's pension, which is all we live on now apart from Nay's picture sales. I'm sorry, but I have to say no."

"Oh, well, no big deal, Unc. Just thought I'd ask, since we were passing by, and I thought you've love to meet Suze."

"Oh, it's been a great pleasure." I said, "Charming girl. I'm sure something'll turn up."

"Yeah, I'm sure it will."

His eyes scanned the room.

"This you're collection? Dad was telling us about it. Old boxes, right?"

He rummaged through my display of treasures. Suze sat on the terrace, looking at the river, still bored.

"This one's my favourite." I said and picked the Chinese puzzle box to show him how it worked, but he'd spotted something else of interest.

"This must be worth a pretty penny." He said, holding the golden Faerie bowl.

"Well, it is unique. It was a present from some special friends." I said.

He turned away and called to his girlfriend. "Come on, Suze. We'd better get back on the road. Thanks, Uncle," he said as he let himself out, "Might pop in on our way back to show off my pretty new arms."

"Most unlikely." I thought. "Have a good trip, Nathan. I hope the treatment's a success. Bye Suze."

I waved them off and returned to my treasures, to rearrange the display. I noticed the Faerie bowl was missing.

"Shit!"

I rushed to the door, down the steps to the ferry quay, but Nathan's boat had sailed. He and Suze were standing by their car. "Nathan!" I shouted and waved my arms in frustration. He waved back with a big smiley face. "Nice to see you Uncle Tom!" He called.

When Naomi came home, I told her what happened.

"I'm sure he didn't mean to take it." She said.

"It's hard to steal a valuable golden bowl accidentally."

"Oh well, Mother always said, 'Nothing good ever comes of a bad deed.' Naomi unpacked her shopping.

So, now, one week later, I've received a postcard, addressed to *"Will's Uncle Tom, The House by the River Dart, Big Ferry."* The picture is of the lighthouse on Plymouth Hoe.

It's in the tiniest handwriting which fills the message space and then spirals around the address and the stamp. Here's what it said. I hope you understand all the acronyms. I don't. I've corrected the spelling and punctuation – sorry, I couldn't resist.

Dear Uncle Tom,

This is Suze. I hope you remember me from our visit. I thought I should tell you about Nat.

First, I'm not his GF no more. I've had it. He's a PITA, and he's gone too far.

I'm sure you've realised by now, he nicked your gold bowl. I didn't think it was fair, you being so old and poor and all. So, I told him to go back on the ferry and return it. No use. He said, "You don't turn away a turn-up." Whatever that means.

I bet you knew all that crap about his skin treatment was crap. We came to Plymouth to meet his old mate Tone who's a chef on a big private yacht. Anyway, Tone called Nat to say he had a good stash of C. He'd sell it to Nat for a good price if he could get down quick to do a deal.

When it came to it, Nat had no cash, so he gave Tone your gold dish instead. Turns out Tone really liked it. He gave Nat the package and we just got in the car, when he comes running over yelling his head off, calling Nat dirty words I don't think I should write down in full.

He said what the F-ing, C-ing, F- is this? Then he held out his hand. It was full of dust or soil or something. Nat said, What's that? Tone said it's your F-ing, C-ing unique and valuable antique gold bowl.

Well, there was a big row and a bit of a fight. Nat didn't want to give the stash back, said he'd paid for it in good faith, so Tone decided to kill him right there. Nat got beaten up good, and left empty-handed. I think it's taught him a lesson. He was still confused about it all when I dumped him.

Thought you should know. Soz about the bowl, Unk. Life sucks, dunnit. Suze x

I climbed the cliff to see Sapphire, to confess that my

nephew had stolen her golden bowl.

"I know," she said, "We saw the boy hide it in his rucksack. Do not worry, he will learn a valuable lesson."

"He already has," I said, "it turned to dust, and he got beaten by his drug-dealer pal."

"That was his first lesson. He has learned more since. Faerie friends near London visited him last night and whispered dreams about Faerie gold. He now questions his view of reality. His mind is opening to wondrous possibilities."

"Word gets around fast in Faerie circles!" I joked.

"I told you all Faeries see, hear and feel what any one of us experiences. We have a mind we share with Faeries around this country and around the world."

"That's remarkable." I said.

"Many creatures have the same" Sapphire said," – bees, wasps, ants, flocks of starlings, schools of mackerel, swarms of locusts. They move as One. Have you seen the starlings fly in their thousands, their wings almost touching? They sway and rise and fall and make beautiful shapes in the air. They are of a single mind. They are One." Sapphire said.

"The trees in the forest are One. Their roots and fungi link them. They carry nutrients for trees in need, send warnings of danger, cries for help. They create a safe and pleasant place to grow, cool, damp, sheltered from the wind.

The forest is One. Each tree is an organ of the forest body."

"Once every species had its One mind, even humans. But humans were made with a flaw. They were destructive of their own kind. Not like birds who will kill one of their own, if it is sick, for the greater good of the species. Humans kill to satisfy their individual greed."

"Humans found they could use what they know of each other's thoughts to dominate and enslave. So, people learned to hide their thoughts. They used language to say aloud what they wanted their listeners to hear and to hide what they were thinking."

"You humans used your communal mind – the loving, caring mind, less and less. Eventually, you lost the ability to access your species mind. That is why your lives had to be shortened. Your prehistoric forebears lived for thousands of years. But later the Angels saw humans became greedy, aggressive, and dangerous. You became so powerful that your bad decisions could threaten all life on Earth. So, the Angels limited the life of each man and woman, so you could do a maximum of fifty years of active harm or good."

"Since then, the Dreamtime Spirits have been watching over you and helping you appreciate what you had lost. They have seen many of you striving to return to the One and have been rewarding your enlightenment with longevity. You now have up to one hundred years."

"Is the One lost to us forever?" I asked.

"Oh no. It is still there. In fact, there are humans all around the world who can tune to it through prayer and meditation. I could show you how."

"I would love that."

"Well, I did promise I would take you there before your Earth time ends. Let us go now."

"Listen only to me, Thomas." Sapphire said, "Close your eyes. Think about nothing but your breathing. Imagine you are in a long tunnel. Tell me what you see."

"I see a long tunnel."

"That is a good start. Fly down the tunnel. What do you see at the end of the tunnel?"

"There is a white light."

"Fly towards the light."

"I'm trying. The tunnel's getting longer. I'm getting no closer."

"Keep flying towards it. What colour is the light now?"

"It's bluish."

"Keep flying towards the light."

"It's a long way."

"Keep flying. What colour is the light now?"

"It's sky blue."

"Keep flying. What colour is the light now?"

"It's deeper blue like sapphires."

"And now?"

"It's indigo, purple. It's very deep."

"Now fly into the light. What is happening now?"

"I'm in the light, surrounded."

"You are in the One. Stay as long as you wish."

"I'm melting."

I felt I had no body. I was nobody. I was One with the deep blue, floating, pulsing gently with the heartbeat of the Universe. I was totally absorbed into the light.

I was connected with everything – every human every species, plant and animal, every being, every object and force – the wind the sky, the water, the earth, the stars. I was connected with all beings which are One being. I knew everything – the past present and the future, all One, all here now, always. I knew that my world, my life, and all the lives on Earth were stories. Life and death, sickness and pain, poverty and wealth, joy and despair – they are all illusions. They are as thin as mist. It's all a dream among the billions of dreams we all dream.

I felt that every creature was part of me, and I was part of it. There were no tribes, no countries, no borders. One thing tied everything and every being together – an overwhelming sense of love. We are all expressions of the One Love, which is above the love of lovers, wives, children, sisters, friends, neighbours, compatriots, above the love of beliefs, ideals, loyalties, above morality, above judgement.

I knew there is One God, and it is We. We are God and God is us. We created the Universe, and we are its creation. We dreamed the Universe, and we continue to dream it – all of us together.

I floated for a second or an hour or a year, without time, without thought. I felt safe in the hands of the One in the infinite deepest blue.

I opened my eyes and woke to a spectacular and beautiful world of wonder. I was in a forest, in a sunny clearing. Everything was pulsing with super-colours, as if lit from within, a million shades of leafy green, watery silvers and sky blues. The kaleidoscope of colour resolved into distinct forms, trees, bushes, flowers, clouds, a stream under a fall of boughs, a huge standing Oak. All were distinct while all being One, and I was One with it all.

A cloud of Faeries appeared before me and I felt a great love for them, a love beyond time, that began with the birth of the Universe and continues to forever. Sapphire Silverwings emerged from the Faerie cloud. I felt immense gratitude for her and all her kind, who gave me this astonishing gift. I opened my mouth to thank her.

"Do not speak." She said, finger to her lips. "Do not move. Do not think. Just observe as you return to your Self."

I was full of awe at the beauty of the world. After a while, the heightened perception began to fade and the forest returned to its everyday colours. I slid back fully into my body and felt a twinge in my aching back.

Sapphire smiled with great understanding. "Do not worry, Thomas. Now you have touched the One, you will never again be just one human. You know it is there. You can return at any time. Just conjure the tunnel, fly towards the deepest blue, and you will find it."

I wanted to tell Naomi of the wonders I'd just experienced. But I knew, I wouldn't be able the find the words. When I saw her, I yearned to hold her close to me and tell her that I loved her deeply, and that everything would be all right. I wanted to say, despite all that seemed bad between us, our love is eternal, and all will be good.

I held my hand out to her and for the first time in a long long while, she took it. We looked into each other's eyes and connected, silently. She smiled.

That was enough for now.

I went to my workshop to finish the puzzle box I'd been making for Sapphire's Journal.

When I saw Sapphire today, she greeted me with a prayer-hands gesture. I did the same. I understood we were acknowledging the experience we had shared yesterday. There was nothing we needed to say. We were silent for minutes. Sapphire opened her hands.

From my rucksack, I took the box I'd made for the Journal and placed it on the grass before her. I said, "I am sorry it has taken me so long to make. I designed it to be more fiendishly difficult than any I've made before."

Sapphire hovered above it for a few minutes.

I waited nervously.

"Clever!" She said at last, "It is a work of a genius!"

"Well, thank you." I said, relieved.

"But let us make it even more of a challenge for Willow."

I'd decorated the box with inlays of contrasting wood, like the pencil box I made for Willow.

"Let's give her no clues at all." Sapphire said.

She floated in circles around the box, singing a very high note, that echoed inside my head. Very soon, I noticed the inlaid wood pattern had fused into a smooth surface of plain mahogany. The sides and corners of the box had melted into perfect curves.

The surface glazed over until it looked like a solid block of highly polished hardwood. I took it in my hands. It felt super smooth, without a mark or a join. Even the grain pattern in the wood had disappeared. It was like highly polished glass.

"That's wonderful, but will I still be able to open it?"

"Yes," Sapphire said, "your muscle memory will find all the buttons and slides."

"And Willow?"

"She will share the memory of your movements, which are now locked forever in the wood. She will not know how she opened the box, and no other human on Earth will be able to do the same."

12

It would be impossible to live in Quay Cottage without falling under the spell of the river and its rhythms: The sunrise filtering through the oaks high in the Hoodown Woods and the sunset over the roofs of the Britannia Royal Naval College. The moonrise over the homely lights of Kingswear and the moon setting into its reflection in Old Mill Creek.

We were always conscious of the ebb and flow of the tide. High Spring tides with the river flooding the ferry slipway, drowning our little beach and filling the house with reflected sky light, and the low neap tide depositing its flotsam for Naomi, our daily beachcomber. The lowest tides exposed the inter-tidal mud, attracting the wading egrets, oyster catchers, shelducks, and the fishermen who came to harvest the soft-shell crabs for bait.

This morning, Naomi and Willow were beach-combing by the river in front of the house. I shouted from the terrace, "What did you find?" Willow hefted an armful of driftwood and Naomi showed off a bin bag of treasure she'd collected from the ankle-deep carpet of drying seaweed, flotsam, and jetsam.

"Two Coke bottles, one lemonade, a plastic cup, polystyrene packaging, plastic bags, a fender, some blue tarpaulin, a panty liner. There's lots more out there. Too much for us to clear. It'll take hours."

"We need a storm." I said.

"Humph!" Naomi grunted. She hated storms.

She dumped the rubbish in the public litter bin by the slipway. Willow stacked the driftwood, which we used for garden fencing, in a pile in the yard. Naomi tied the fender to the side of the log store, with a dozen fenders she'd previously salvaged to festoon around the garden.

Willow ran to the house waving something. "Papa, Papa, look!" she shouted. She ran in and sat between me, Roland and Gemma.

"I found a doll."

She waved a plastic doll, dressed in traditional Irish costume.

"She's Irish, like Grandma Nay." She passed it to her mother.

"That must've been lost by a little girl and then ended up in the river." Gemma said, "Perhaps she took one of the steamer trips up to Totnes, and it fell overboard."

"Can we go on a steamer trip? Can we do the Round Robin?" Willow asked.

"Good idea," Roland said, "but right now, we need to get ready for our sleepover on the boat."

The boat was Joe Shepherd's third surprise gift. When Joe handed us the house keys, there was a note attached to the key ring. Joe wrote, *"Read this after I'm gone."* When he had driven away on the ferry to his new life in County Kerry,

Naomi opened the note. She read:

"Tom and Naomi, Here's the key to your new boat. It's a 44-year-old, 25ft Gaff Cutter that came with the name Angel. You can see her from the cottage, just downstream on the trots. I've had her 20 years. Now she's yours – no charge. You gave me a very fair price for the house, and I couldn't let you live by the river without a boat. Go see Mr. Grumpy the Harbour Master and register it in your name. Tell the old bastard I'll truly miss him. — Joe"

The gift of the boat was a considerable surprise. Neither of us are natural sailors. I'm too lazy for all the maintenance and Naomi, although a County Cork team swimmer as a child, was never happy being in deep water when she didn't know what lay beneath. She'd had nightmares about drowning as a child, something she inherited from her mother, and grandmother, who were also scared of drowning. So, we handed the boat over to Roland and Gemma, who were delighted, and took every opportunity to sail, picnic or spend a night moored on the water.

"Yaaay!" Willow shouted. She loved sleeping over on the boat. It was so cozy. It had four beds, so Willow slept in two of them. A Calor gas heater kept it nice and warm.

They went off to collect their boat shoes, overnight bags, picnic food and life jackets. We waved goodbye from the terrace. They walked along the railway path to take their tender over to Angel, which was moored just fifty yards out, on the nearby trots.

"Have fun. See you tomorrow. Breakfast at nine." Naomi shouted from the terrace. She turned to me and said, "I do worry about them."

I said, "What's to worry about? The weather report's OK. They're moored up, safe. Only fifty yards out. They've got the tender. They can zip back if it gets windy. Tell you what, Nay, leave the door unlocked for them."

We came inside and looked from the terrace window. We surveyed the sky all around, from to Old Mill Creek, to the river mouth, back to the Kingswear side, the Hoodown woods. All was calm. I noticed Willow's dove perched on Joe's Faerie's head. The dove flew down towards us and fluttered against the pane, right in our faces. I drew back and the dove retreated to the woods. Naomi and I looked at each other, puzzled. We only ever saw the dove when Willow was around and we'd never seen it so agitated.

"I'll put a hot botty in their bed. Just in case." Naomi said.

I stayed to watch the ferry loading.

I'd grown to love the charming Higher Ferry. It was originally called the Floating Bridge because Alexander Kingdom Brunel, who built the railway from Paignton, aimed to build a bridge across to Dartmouth. Unfortunately, he couldn't raise the investment so the railway ran on to Kingswear village, on our side of the river. Brunel built a terminus and laid on a passenger ferry to take people across the river from Kingswear Station to Dartmouth.

That wasn't convenient enough for the Commander of the Britannia Royal Navy College, which lies across the river, opposite us. He thought the Navy cadets, coming down from Exeter or London, might get distracted by the sleazy distractions of Dartmouth if they continued to the station, and took the Lower Ferry into town, so he built Britannia Halt below Quay Cottage. When the train stopped at the

Halt, the sailors could jump on to Navy launches to be ferried across. Later, under an Act of Parliament, a public ferry took over the job, and they called it the Floating Bridge.

The current incarnation of the ferry is a wide, drive-on-drive-off platform with hydraulic lifting prowls at each end. It's push-me-pull-you diesel-electric motors drive twelve-foot paddle wheels, which shuttle it back and forth across the Dart.

The vessel and its cargo of up to sixteen cars, a few motorbikes and a handful of foot passengers, is held on course between two one-inch thick wires. These are secured on each river bank by concrete counterweights housed in deep cylinders buried in the slipways. The rusty wires run through pulleys on each side of the ferry.

It wasn't just the wires that were rusting, the ferry, though quaint and much cherished as a historic treasure of the town, was showing its age. The engines were tired, noisy, and inefficient and the rotting hull had become too expensive to maintain and repair, so its days were numbered. One hundred and fifty days, in fact, until its replacement with a new hi-tech ferry that was being built in Holland. With each crossing, it was chugging slowly towards the scrapyard.

That night, we got the storm I'd innocently wished for. It had been building through the evening, and by midnight a force nine northerly was roaring down the river, driving heavy rain horizontally, pushing three-foot waves and whipping spray from their crests. It was the worst storm we'd seen. We stood at the riverside window watching the yachts rocking wildly on the trots. The wind howled through their rigging and thrashed at their masts, which swayed like crazy metronomes.

I heard Sapphire's voice in my head. *"Thomas, the children are in danger. They must leave the boat!"*

I shouted, "Nay, We must get them off the boat."

"B'Jesus, Tom! They didn't give this on the radio. This looks bad." She said, "Terrible!"

When the tide is running fast, it can push the ferry sideways, upstream or downstream, and the ferry strains on its wires and crosses the river in a great arc. Tonight, the outgoing high spring tide, was bending the ferry's path downriver. The unprecedented gale, gusting from the north at 70 miles per hour, was buffeting the topsides, which acted like a massive sail. The ferry, with its metal and human cargo, was beam-on to the storm, with wind and tide working together to put huge strain on the rusty wires.

We watched as the slowly advancing ferry reached mid-river. The wires were stretched to their limit like an archer's bowline fully drawn with the ferry held like an arrow under tension, straining to fly off downstream. The feeble paddles driven at full speed made a deal of splash, but no progress.

The ferry was stuck, with the wires, at fifty degrees to the ferry, creating a virtual fence that prevented any headway across the river. It couldn't move forwards or backwards. The irresistible forces of the gale and the tide opposed the immovable object of the ferry.

We heard a loud crack, a thunderbolt. The nearest end of the downstream ferry cable was yanked from its concrete counterweight. It snaked murderously into the turbulent air and whipped into the river, sending up a line of spray.

"Oh my God!" Naomi screamed.

The ferry was now restrained only by the upstream wire –

but in a few seconds a gust hit the topsides, and the wire, like its sister, broke free, twisted in the air and slashed across the ferry prowl. It was quickly drawn through the runners and sank into the river.

With no restraining wires, the ferry lurched to port and floated off downstream towards the trot lines which held fifty moored yachts including the Angel.

We looked at each other open-mouthed.

I heard Sapphire's voice again. *"Come to the boat, Thomas! Come to the boat!"*

"Come on, Nay! The Faeries!" I shouted. "We must help the kids!" I leapt down the stairs with Naomi close behind.

We threw on our sailing jackets and woolen hats. Naomi grabbed the torch we kept by the door, and we pushed into the driving wind and rain. I ran to the workshop and grabbed the rescue line and lifebelt and chased after Naomi who was speeding down the railway path towards the moorings.

With the rain in my eyes, I couldn't see the ferry, but I could hear the creaks and cracks above the roar of the wind, as it lumbered into one yacht and then another, ripping their mooring lines and cracking them into shards of fibre glass, which were whipped away seaward by the wind.

We reached the Angel and Naomi pointed the torch towards it. We saw Willow emerge from the cabin, followed closely by Roland and Gemma as the ferry was bearing down upon their flimsy boat.

They were being thrown about wildly, confused and frightened. Willow was frantically pointing at the ferry, its paddles thrashing the water in full reverse, trying to slow its lethal trajectory. It was thirty feet upstream, heading sideways towards their yacht.

Naomi directed the torch at Roland and Gemma and then at the ferry. Roland and Gemma turned to see the churning paddles, now just twenty feet from their faces. There was much shouting and waving of arms and a scrabbling for the tender, a two-metre inflatable, tied to the yacht. They fell in and Roland released the painter.

The wind snatched the dinghy and thrust it free from the yacht, just as the port paddle wheel ground into the yacht's stern. It ripped the outboard from its mountings, smashed the rudder and tiller and then tore into the cockpit.

The weight of the ferry and its cargo of cars supplemented by the force of wind and tide were enough to snap the yacht's mooring lines. The ferry drifted sideways into the yacht and pushed it towards the Kingswear bank.

The little dinghy bounced violently against the riverbank, with our terrified family gripping the gunwale lines with both hands. The banks were four meters high and clad with vertically coursed stone slates, designed to protect the railway from the river's erosion. Now, half an hour past high tide, there were just two metres of wall exposed, but it was wet and slippery and almost impossible to climb.

I secured my end of the rescue rope around a concrete railway fencepost behind me and shouted, "Grab this!". I threw the lifebelt down to the dinghy

Roland reached for it but missed as the wind whipped it away. He tried twice more and caught the ring. He wrestled it over Willow's head and arms. She grabbed the rope in both hands, sat on the gunwales and when the dinghy swung towards the bank she aimed both feet at the wall. But her boat shoes had no grip on the algae-slicked stone, and she fell against the wall, half submerged in the freezing water. The ring cushioned her fall a little, but her hips smashed into the wet stone. She yelled but held her grip.

Naomi and I pulled against the rope and Willow began to scramble up until Naomi, lying face down on the path, could reach out and grab the back of her life jacket and pull her up. Poor Willow had no energy left. She just rolled away from the edge and lay, shaking and sobbing.

Gemma had better luck and caught the ring first time and pulled it over her head. She worked her feet into a good climbing position and pulled hand over hand up the rope. Roland did the same. He was stronger and able to climb quickly, even though the wind twice snatched at his feet and swung him against the wall.

As we dragged Roland over the edge of the path, we heard a mighty crash and grinding of metal. The ferry and what was left of Angel, went shuddering along the river wall, towards the dinghy. In seconds, the dinghy was sucked under the prowl and the ferry slid past, the paddle wheels grounding against the rocky river bank. In twenty yards it twisted to port, the prowl reared up and mounted the wall. The ferry came to a stop.

When our exhausted, drenched and frozen family were ready to move, We helped them back to the cottage. In the warmth of the house, Naomi draped them in towels. I brought hot chocolate for Willow and tea for Roland and Gemma and I stoked the fire. Naomi ran a hot bath and led all three to the bathroom and left them to it.

I called the police to tell them about the ferry, but they'd already had dozens of calls and said the coastguard and navy were securing the ferry and evacuating passengers.

Willow, when she was warm again, came and sat by the

fire with Naomi and me, cradling her hot chocolate. "Papa," She said, "they saved us. It was the Faeries. They came to me, Papa. We were bumping about in the boat. They made this whistling noise outside. I popped my head through the hatch, and they danced around me in a cloud. Then the cloud opened in the middle and I saw the ferry and I shouted Mummy and Daddy to come out. The Faeries saved us, Grandma!"

Naomi gave Willow a big hug. "Yes. They warned Grandpa too. I thought we might lose you." She said through tears.

"No, Grandma, the Faeries promised they would look after all of us, and they did."

Naomi said, "Hmm! I think it's about time I met your Faerie friends."

Willow and I exchanged silent glances.

"But Grandma, you always laugh about them."

"That doesn't mean I don't respect them." Naomi said.

I said, "Naomi, you won't be able to see or hear them at first. It took a long time building trust before they gave me the Seeing and the Hearing."

"If that's the case, you can tell me what they look like and what they say. Take me to see them."

13

I was overwhelmed with gratitude to the Faeries for delivering my precious family from the blades of the paddle wheel. I wanted to take Naomi and Willow up the cliff straight away to thank them, but the night was still wild, and my family needed attention. Our thanks had to wait until morning.

When we woke, the storm had subsided. Naomi's beach had been swept clean, and the Higher Ferry lay sprawled on the mud like a morning-after drunk.

We had a quick breakfast and Willow told her parents we were off to see the Faeries. They laughed and Gemma said, "Enjoy your walk. Don't lose Roo in the woods."

We were an excited expedition. Willow was thrilled that Naomi would meet Sapphire for the first time. I, too, was excited but nervous about that. Roo was excited by everything.

Naomi puffed a bit and, in places, needed both of us to help her up the cliff. "You do this every day?" She exclaimed. "It's the honey." I laughed.

When we arrived at the Faerie Glen, Sapphire and her sisters flew out to greet us.

Naomi stared, her mouth open in wonder.

Sapphire flew straight to her and hovered before her.

Naomi stared. "Oh My!" She cried, looking back to Willow and me. She was flustered. "I've heard so much about Faeries, from my mother, but I've never actually seen a real one before!" She said, "And now, hundreds!"

"I am Sapphire. These are my sisters. We are delighted to meet you again."

"I'm Nay… Nay… Naomi." She stuttered, "Pleased to meet you."

The Fairies, danced in a circle in the air and sang, "Nay, Nay, Naomi. Nay, Nay, Naomi." To a tune resembling an Irish jig.

Roo joined in the singing. Naomi laughed, eyes open in wonder, "They're spectacular, Tom! Why didn't you invite me sooner!" Willow jumped up and down. I sighed with relief.

Naomi turned to me, "You said I wouldn't be able to see them or talk to them, but I can! May I say thank you?"

"Of course," I said.

"Erm… Miss Sapphire…" She said.

"Just Sapphire will be fine."

"Er… Sapphire, I've come to thank you for saving my granddaughter and Roland and Gemma. They would all have drowned last night if you hadn't warned Willow and Tom."

"And if you had not courageously pulled them from the river." Sapphire said.

"Well, I thank you from the bottom of my heart." Naomi said.

"Well, Naomi, there has been too much drowning in your

family. We could not bear to see any more."

The Faeries danced around us singing, "Nay, Nay, Naomi." Then disappeared into the tree.

Sapphire shot a glance at Roo, who barked, decided this was a good time for a run and dragged his lead from my hand. Willow ran after him. "Come back Roo-Roo!" She shouted, "Naughty boy!"

We all turned to watch her skip after the dog.

"Willow is a most precious child." Sapphire said.

Naomi said, "She is our joy!"

Sapphire continued, "A Twice Born."

Naomi stepped back a pace. I put my hand on her shoulder. She shrugged me off.

"Excuse me, Miss Sapphire, but what do you mean?" She asked.

"I think you know." Sapphire said.

Naomi shook her head in puzzlement.

"When the Angels brought your Daisy Lee, all did not turn out right." Sapphire said.

Naomi clasped her hand to her mouth. "How do you know this?" Naomi said through the start of tears. She looked accusingly at me.

Sapphire said, "We were there, Naomi, at Daisy's birth, with the Angels, to bless your baby. But it went wrong."

"You don't have to tell me that!" Naomi glared at me.

Sapphire said, "For a baby to grow right, millions of cells must sing in harmony. Unfortunately, that did not happen for your child. A few cells went awry. Her body grew twisted and weak. If she had lived, she would have suffered a world of pain. You and Thomas would have lived with heartache throughout your baby's short life."

"Did you... take her away?" Naomi asked.

"Found him!" Willow shouted from the trees. She bounded towards us over exposed roots and fallen boughs, like a young deer.

Willow danced ahead down the hill, singing "Nay, Nay, Naomi. Nay, Nay, Naomi."

Naomi hesitated and glanced through her tears at Sapphire.

Willow circled back and grabbed Naomi's hand. "Come on, Grandma." She said and dragged her away.

Back at the cottage, Willow noticed Naomi looked concerned. "You all right, Grandma?" She said.

Naomi snapped out of her retrospection. "I'm fine, me darlin' girl." She said, with a playful Irish lilt and a smile for Willow and her parents.

Willow said, "Mummy, Daddy, Grandma saw the Faeries. They gave her a new name. Nay Nay Naomi!"

Naomi looked at me, alarmed. Roland and Gemma raised their eyebrows and glanced at each other. Their youthful cynicism was unbreakable.

Naomi swiftly left the room and returned with her fiddle. She nodded to me. I nodded back, remembering how she would pick up her fiddle whenever little Willow got upset or overexcited. She would use music to calm her down. I called it her instrument of mass distraction.

Willow said, "Oh, Grandma, Will you play for us? Please?"

Naomi said, "I've got a new tune. I made it for you all. It's called, 'The Rotting Hulk'."

"It's about me." I joked. The kids looked to the ceiling. "Daddy joke." Roland said.

"It's about an old abandoned ship." Naomi said and took up her bow. She played a beautiful lament.

She conjured up the coast of Mull, the old wreck slowly decaying into wild nature. We were all transported by the rhythm of the waves washing over the hull, the melodic cries of gulls wheeling above. They sang of lost times, lost men, lost loves, lost and wandering souls.

That night, for the first time in many years, Naomi came to me and said "Goodnight." before she went to her bed.

Today Naomi and I climbed to the Glen.

Sapphire greeted us.

"Naomi. It is a joy to see you both again. There is a conversation we did not finish."

Naomi took a deep breath looking at the ground she blurted out: "Did you… take Daisy Lee away? It's just that Mother used to say Faeries took human babies. When my grandmother was old, she told stories about the Beautiful Folk. She said she remembered playing with them when she was small. She said she followed after the Faeries. Well, did you… take my Daisy Lee?"

Sapphire said, "Such a decision is not for Faeries."

"But we prayed so hard for her! We prayed to God to spare her!" Naomi pleaded tearfully.

I avoided Sapphire's eyes and looked to the ground, remembering what I had prayed for.

"Your God did spare her, Naomi. God spared her from a life of pain and ordered the Angels to take her." Sapphire said.

Naomi sobbed.

"Now is not the time for weeping. That time is long past." Sapphire said, "Thomas, Naomi, you both wished only the best for your child. Her fate was in the hands of others superior to you and to we Faerie Folk. The Angels took back the soul you called Daisy Lee. We took her pain away at the end. We sang her a lullaby. She slipped away in peace."

"Thank you." Naomi said.

"And now you have Willow."

"She was such a Godsend." Naomi said, sniffling. "As soon as I held that darling child in my arms, it was as if we had our little Daisy back!"

"You did have Daisy back." Sapphire said.

Naomi glanced at me, confused.

"When the Angels took Daisy away," Sapphire continued, "they listened to Thomas's prayer."

"He prayed for her to die!" Naomi cried. "He wanted her dead. Three times he betrayed that poor child. First, he wanted an abortion. Then he prayed for her to be still born and when she was born alive, he prayed that God would still take her. She had just ten minutes! He's like Peter. He denied Jesus three times before cock crow."

Sapphire said, "Yes it is true, Thomas did that Naomi."

Naomi shot me a hateful look.

Sapphire said, "He prayed to save Daisy and you from a lifetime of pain. But he also prayed for your God to give you another healthy child to take her place. That is the prayer that God and the Angels heard, and that is the prayer they answered."

Naomi looked at me confused.

"Come with me." Sapphire said, "Both of you."

"Where to?" Naomi asked.

"Not where, but when." Sapphire said. "Please hold hands."

I reached out for Naomi. She pulled back, then reluctantly took both my hands. She looked frightened.

"It will be all right." I said

Sapphire said. "You will both remember something you have lived through but did not entirely witness. Please close your eyes."

We obeyed. A grey cloud enveloped us both and darkened to the black of night. I could still see Naomi staring into my eyes. We both became dizzy and weak and clung on to each other. The darkness dissipated, and we were back in the maternity room, looking down from a corner of the ceiling.

The Naomi in front of me, holding my hands, looked into my eyes beseechingly and screamed, "Save my baby! Save my baby!"

She turned to look at Naomi on the bed, who screamed, "Save my baby! Save my baby!"

We both saw Thomas sitting beside the bed, holding Naomi's hands, looking into her eyes with deep compassion, tears streaming down his face.

We both heard, aloud, the prayer inside his head. "Please God, save our little Daisy Lee from a life of pain and sorrow. Please, Please God, I beg you to take Daisy back to Heaven right now and bring Naomi another healthy child."

As the dark cloud enveloped us again, Naomi held me tight and the blackness came.

"Open your eyes." Sapphire said.

We were back in the grassy clearing, still clinging to each other. Naomi cried, "Oh Tom! I didn't know!"

Sapphire said: "The Angels heard Thomas's prayer. They waited for you to be with child again. They waited to bring another baby for you and Thomas."

Naomi said, "You tried for years to convince me to have another baby, but I couldn't sleep with you. I couldn't even touch you. When I looked at you, I saw a wicked man who wanted an abortion, a still birth and then prayed again for your child to die after ten minutes of life."

Sapphire said: "When the Angels saw you could not be with child, they waited for another opportunity."

"Opportunity for what?" Naomi said.

"To bring Daisy's spirit back."

Naomi frowned.

"When your son and his wife were ready, and the Universe was ready, and the year had turned inside out, from 47 to 74, the Angels brought Daisy to them."

Naomi looked from me to Sapphire. "I don't understand." She said.

"It happened here in the Forest." Sapphire said, "We drew Roland and Gemma to the Willow tree, where they lay together. At the conception, the Angels brought the Spirit of Daisy back into the world. We blessed the child with a Faerie nature, and we gave her a new name for a new life. Willow!"

Naomi shouted, "A Twice Born, you said, Twice Born!"

She clasped her hand to her open mouth. She was breathing heavily. Her legs gave way, she swayed and fell to the ground. I put my arms around her. She looked up at me, tears streaming.

"Oh, Tom! You did it! You prayed for her to come again!" She sobbed, "And God heard you, and the Angels heard you, and they brought her back. Our Daisy. Our Willow!"

She grabbed me. "Will you ever forgive me, Tom? I thought…"

I held her close and she hugged me tight.

"All these years." She said, "I thought…"

"Shhh!" I whispered.

"Oh Tom!" She said, "I am so sorry!"

"You need some time together," Sapphire said.

I thought, *"Life is brutal."*

Sapphire nodded and thought, *"And life is beautiful."*

Naomi took my hand and said through her tears: "Thank you, Sapphire, for everything you have done for me and Tom and my family. Thank you, from the bottom of my heart."

Then she looked at me and said, "Come on, Thomas, Tommy, Tom-Tom, we have things to talk about."

Back at the cottage, Naomi went straight to Willow. Naomi hugged her, lifted her off her feet, spun her round and round and said, "Oh me darlin' girl."

Willow, surprised but delighted, said, "Play for us Grandma, before we go home."

Naomi took up her fiddle and played a happy reel. Willow took my hand, and she swayed like the branches of a Willow tree, in a summer breeze.

This morning, I felt Naomi's arms around me. She came to my bed in the night. When I opened my eyes, she was already awake, looking at me. She said, "Tom, you know, we never stopped loving each other, did we? It's just that the pain kept getting in the way."

"I know, Nay."

"Can you forgive me, Tom? All these years. The things I

thought about you? I blamed you. I refused another baby. I froze you out?"

We cuddled. I said, "Nay, I thought I deserved all of that. I couldn't forgive myself for wanting a child to die."

"God has forgiven the both of us." She said.

At breakfast, she poured and sugared my tea. "One for you. One for me. One for little Daisy Lee." She hesitated a beat, "And one for our darlin' Willow." She smiled.

"Nay, we are so, so lucky the Faeries came to help us." I said.

"Yes..." Naomi said, "I've been wondering about that."

"Hmm?"

"Well, why did they go to all this trouble for us? They made their village here, they coaxed us, whispered us, to this house. They brought Daisy back into the world. They blessed Willow with their gifts. They revealed themselves to her, so she would lead you to them. Why did they tell you their secrets, make you well again. Why you, Tom?"

I shrugged.

"It's because they wanted to talk to me." Naomi said. "They knew Mother was wary of the Fae Folk, as was I. They invited little Willow, and then she invited you. They charmed you with their stories, and they tested you to see if you were honest and true."

"Don't you see? They made a bargain with you and when you kept your promises – kept their secrets and saved them from harm, that's when they asked you to invite me. They wanted me!"

"You clever Faerie." I thought.

"But why me, Tom? Why you? Why Willow? Why us?" She said.

"Why don't you ask them?" I said.

Today, when we saw Sapphire, Naomi said, "I wish to sincerely thank you for opening my eyes."

Sapphire nodded.

"For so many years I've been locked up in my grief. I blamed myself. I blamed Tom. I froze him out for decades. And then to think that for ten years my lost child was right here in front of me! I want to thank you, Sapphire, for helping us."

"That is why we are here." Sapphire said.

"But, please forgive me for asking, why did you come here for us, when there are so many people with problems in this world?"

Sapphire said, "Just as Daisy and Willow were chosen and blessed, you too were chosen. We were invited to bless you, Naomi, at your birth."

"You blessed me?"

"Yes. You, your mother, Eleanor, and your grandmother, Naimh."

"You knew us all?"

"We did, and we protected you all, back five generations to your great grandmother, Bridget O'Ceallaigh of Galway."

Willow's dove flew out of the woods and settled on a branch nearby.

Naomi said, "I've not heard that name before. Grandma always said her mother was Mary, and she grew up in Kinsale."

"That is true, but Mary was not her birth mother." Sapphire said. "There is much to tell, Naomi, and it will be long in the telling. Things have been hidden from you. Are you ready to listen and listen long?"

Naomi looked at me. We both nodded.

"As long as it takes." Naomi said.

Sapphire gestured Naomi to sit by me on the grass.

Sapphire rested on a twig before us and said, "I need to tell you about a mistake we Faerie Folk made, many years ago, and about a promise to a dear friend, Bridget O'Ceallaigh."

Naomi nodded.

"Your great grandmother, Bridget, was just a wisp of a woman, but she had the heart of an oak. She was born in 1840, on Inishmore. When she was an infant, there was no work, so her father moved to the mainland. She grew up in a small fishing village near Galway. She blossomed into a handsome colleen with bright red hair and a free spirit. Her name in Gaelic meant 'bright headed' or 'troublesome'."

"She was a gifted musician, played the fiddle. She played more than music. She played joy and good health to all who heard her. She would play at the pub for the fishermen when they returned battered and exhausted for the sea. Her music would lift them up, So they were fighting fit and ready for their next sailing."

"Her first husband was a fisherman. He drowned in a storm before they could get with child. She was pursued by a younger man and married again before her widow's mourning time was over. That did not endear her to the Priest."

"It was a dreadful, hard life for fisherfolk. Bridget's second husband was also taken in a storm, but she gave birth eight months later to a boy. She adored her baby and took great care of him, but he contracted the dysentery and became very ill. She could not afford to pay the Doctor from

Galway, and she did not know how to help the baby. She could only watch her child die."

"As I did." Naomi looked down.

"In her grief," Sapphire continued, "Bridget would wander alone in the wild places, where she found us. She loved our Faerie Folk, and we became good friends. We asked her to help us care for the villagers.

We taught her to heal with plants and fungi. In time, she became very skilled. She helped the sick in the village, particularly the babies and infants and those the Doctor failed to cure. Many would have died without her. The people loved their Biddy. She never took their money. They paid her with fresh-caught fish, potatoes, firewood, and potcheen."

"She took a third husband who gave her a baby girl, your grandmother. She called her baby Niamh, meaning 'brightness' and she cherished her as the most precious thing in her life. With her healing skills, Bridget kept the child from sickness and the baby thrived."

"Bridget played soft airs on her fiddle for Niamh at bedtime and the music would waft from the windows in the evening air. Everybody smiled as they walked past her cottage and felt a little more joy, without knowing why."

"In the mornings, Bridget would wake little Niamh from slumber with a fiddle tune and the toddler would dance and sing along with her mother."

"She called her Niamh. Like Naomi?"

"Yes, we whispered Eleanor to give you that name for the memory of your grandmother."

Sapphire continued: "To the Priest and the Doctor, Bridget O'Ceallaigh was as troublesome as her name, and they wanted her gone. When an infant died of the dysentery, the

Doctor told Mrs Doherty at the village shop that he saw Biddy O'Ceallaigh outside the dead child's house. Mrs Doherty told customers Biddy was staring in the window the night the child died."

"When the catch was poor, Patrick Quinn, the fisherman with the worst haul, said he saw Biddy staring at his boat and mumbling before he set to sea. Soon the men were saying she'd cursed his catch."

"The winter storms came and her third husband, and three crewmen, drowned when the sea took their boat. Tongues wagged. 'Three husbands, all drowned in storms, one after t'other. Makes you think, don't it!'"

"The good Doctor whispered to Katy, the barmaid in O'Conner's, that Biddy talked to faeries and soon word spread that she talked to the Devil himself. Village folk said she was a witch and that's why she only had children by dead men. Others said she slept with the Devil and her red-haired daughter was the Devil's own."

"That's terrible." Naomi said.

"The rumours grew more extreme with each telling." Sapphire said, "Until a great fear of the witch's evil eye spread throughout the countryside around."

"The Priest gave a sermon, warning all good Catholics to reject and expose the false healers and the trickery they had learned from the Devil. 'For they will pretend to save one of your sick to steal your gratitude, money and gifts, while cursing three of your healthy ones to die in pain. That is their payback to the Devil. I beseech you to trust only the God-fearing doctors of science and learning and send the tricksters to join their Master in hell!'"

"The night of the sermon there was a fearsome, powerful

storm. Bridget hated storms. They stole her menfolk away. She cuddled up with Niamh swaddled in blankets on the armchair by the fire."

"You hate storms, Nay." I said. She nodded.

Sapphire continued: "That night, the village baker, Michael Quinn and his wife, Mary, had a mighty row. Their two toddlers were suffering with the dysentery and Mary wanted to call Biddy to help. But Michael had heard all the stories and would not allow Biddy near his children, so he sent his eldest son, Patrick, to ride the storm to Galway with money to pay the learned Doctor to come tend the children."

"Despite the Doctor's best attentions, both infants died that night. Mary Quinn cursed the Doctor for his incompetence, but he protested, 'How can I, a mortal man, fight the work of that She-Devil! Didn't you see her just now passing by the window!'"

"Quinn rushed over to the inn and dragged out two of his pals. They marched to Bridget's cottage and broke down the door. Michael burst into the dark room. He saw Bridget's hair, flaming in the glow of the fire. He grabbed her and threw her out into the storm. Another bully snatched the clinging baby away and kicked her aside. They dragged Bridget down the street to the shore, shouting, 'Kill the witch! Kill the Witch!'"

"Villagers nearby must have heard Bridget's screams and the men shouting, despite the storm. They all knew what was happening, but they locked their doors and stoked their fires."

"The men threw Bridget on the stony beach. They kicked her and beat her, and then stood back and made a sport of stoning her with fist-sized granite cobbles."

Naomi covered her face with her hands.

Sapphire said, "Our people heard her cries and gathered around her. Bridget was screaming, 'Please! Save my baby! Save my baby!'"

Naomi looked at me. I remembered her cries when Daisy died. Willow's dove flew to the ground nearby and quietly pecked for seeds.

Sapphire said, "We made a solemn promise to Bridget O'Ceallaigh that night, as her beautiful spirit was fading from this world. We took away her pain, and we promised we would protect her little girl, and all the girl babies down her generations. Word of that promise spread to all the Faerie folk in Ireland and those beyond. It became an obligation for all Faeries, everywhere."

"Michael threw one last rock at Bridget's head. As she drifted away, she thanked us."

"The men dragged her to the shoreline. They took her arms and feet, waded out. They cast her bleeding body into the ebbing tide and watched the storm take her away."

"Quinn led the men back to Bridget's cottage. They chanted, 'Kill the brat! Kill the brat! Kill the Devil's spawn!' They searched the cottage, but could not find the child. They cursed and returned to the pub."

They told their pals what they had done and drank generous amounts of moonshine.

"Where was the child?" Naomi asked.

"We had reached Bridget's cottage before the murderers. Little Niamh was hiding in a linen box. We lead the child to the back door. We danced and sang to entice her away. She toddled after us with eyes wide, laughing and cooing. We sang:

'Come, child, and see the shining moon.
Come see the twinkling stars.
Come live a wondrous Faerie life.
From now, you will be ours.'"

"We took her on a long journey, away from that village, to the far coast, a place in County Cork, where none would know her and we hoped she would never hear of her poor mother's fate. We found a guardian, Mary O' Hannity, a kindly woman who took the child and cared for her. We watched over Niamh's new family. We blessed her with the Seeing, the Hearing, and the Healing. As she grew, we taught her to cure the sick. After what had happened to her mother, we also taught her to work with subtlety and cunning, so no Priest or Doctor would know who had cured their sick parishioners."

"Niamh had no clear memory of her natural mother, Bridget. She never heard the Galway tale about the drowning of a fisherman's wife whose child was taken by the Faeries. Your mother, Eleanor, suspected something about Niamh's past, but she mostly kept it to herself."

Naomi said, "Mother told me that when Grandma was dying she said, 'They have come for me, Eleanor! The pretty ones. They are singing. Wait for me! Wait for me!'"

"Yes, we were there." Sapphire said.

"And… you kept your promise to Bridget?" Naomi asked.

"We tried," Sapphire said, "We cared for Niamh and blessed her, and we blessed your mother, Eleanor, and we blessed you at your birth. We gave you the Music, Bridget's Music."

"Bridget's Music?"

"Did you never wonder how you could play the fiddle without lessons, or how you knew hundreds of tunes without learning them, or how your music always gave joy and well-being to all who listened?"

Naomi's mouth dropped open and she looked at me. I smiled back.

"We gave you the Artistry, the Seeing, and the Hearing."

"My painting?" Naomi asked.

"Yes, and remember, you could see us and hear us straight away. But then..."

"But then?" Naomi said.

"But then, you lost your Daisy Lee." Sapphire said. "That was a terrible mistake of nature, and it took you both years to recover." Sapphire said. "We brought you and Thomas to live here. We whispered in your dreams with visions of this beautiful place. We nudged you closer and closer until you found the cottage, a place in nature where you could be healed, a safe place where we could protect you and your children."

"But, I watched my child die in my arms." Naomi sobbed.

"And we shared your sadness, Naomi," Sapphire said, "for we had failed to protect a girl child of the generations of Bridget O'Ceallaigh. It took twenty-seven years before we were able to make good our broken promise to Bridget and our obligation to you."

I placed my hand on Naomi's shoulder. She leaned towards me. I said, "Nay, they brought her back. They brought our Willow."

Naomi looked at Sapphire, "You said 'Twice Born.'"

Sapphire smiled.

Willow's dove flew high into the oak tree.

We walked home together. At the top of the stone steps, Naomi gestured for us to sit.

"Tom," She said, "Do you think we should tell Rolly and Gem?"

"About the Faeries? They've been laughing about them all along. They think it's all just a game for Willow."

"No, I mean about Willow… and Daisy?" She said.

"Mmm, a good question." I said.

"I mean," Naomi said, "Rolly is Mister Sensible. He won't believe anything we say about any Faerie folk and I don't think Gemmy, lovely mum as she is, would be able to accept that her daughter is also my daughter. Tom it really would blow her mind!"

"Well," I said, "I promised Sapphire to keep their Faerie secrets for ten years. Willow knows nothing about Daisy and doesn't need to, for now. She won't be able to read the Journal until she comes of age. I think the pages will be blank to her until she's twenty-one. Even then, it won't be public until she somehow shares it with the world. By then we'll be on the other side, and Rolly and Gem will probably think Willow made the whole thing up."

"Or they might be older and wiser, and maybe, ready to appreciate Willow for the miracle that she is."

She turned to me and placed her finger on her lips and said, 'Twice Born – our little secret."

When arrived at the terrace, Willow was helping her parents lay up for lunch. They were all busy, unaware of the drama happening around them.

Naomi smiled and said. "Hey, kids, let's all take the Round Robin tomorrow. It's been such a long time since our last trip."

Roland said, "Sure, Mum. Nice idea."

"Love to!" Gemma said.

"Yay!" Willow danced around the kitchen.

Willow was up early organising everyone for the trip. "Camera, 'noculars, bottle of pop." She stuffed her rucksack.

She helped Naomi butter the bread for the picnic and reminded her Daddy to take ferry money and ticket money. Then off we went to catch the ferry.

"It's the Famous Five!" Willow sang.

"And a dog! And a dog!" Roo barked.

Roland and Gemma walked ahead, swinging arms. Willow shouted, "Come on, Grampses!" She took both our hands and skipped us down the slipway.

Colin the ferryman greeted us with his soft Devon voice.

"Good mornin' young Willow, Thomas, Nay. Are the Archers off on a 'venture?"

"It's Round Robin Day!" Willow sang.

"Thomas and Nay… Round Robin Day.? We're rhymin' are we?" Colin said, taking a biscuit from his pocket for Roo. He looked skyward for inspiration and recited, "Come on across the river wi' me. Then skip along down to the ol' steamer quay!"

Willow sang back: "Up river to Totnes, for a lovely ice cream. Then the bus-top to Paignton. It's just like a dream."

Colin took up the challenge: "A cuppa in the tea shop. Then home on the train. Young Barrie will drive 'ee. In the sun or the rain."

"Yay!" Willow laughed and clapped.

"You wanna be Capt'n, Willow? The boss ain't aboard."

"Love it Mister Colin." She stood straight, saluted and ran ahead through the *Crew Only* gate to the bridge.

Naomi smiled, gave me a big hug and three warm kisses, singing between them, "One for you. One for me. And one for our darlin' Willow."

She squeezed my hand and winked and for the first time, I heard her thinking:

"Twice Born – our little secret."

We laughed as the ferry wheels thrashed at the water and Captain Willow waved from the bridge with Colin's big pilot hat dropped to her nose. I'm not certain, but I think I caught a little wink above her wide grin.

14

This afternoon, Naomi was over the river, shopping. She'd invited me to join her, but I had some Journal writing to catch up with. I said, "You go ahead Nay, I'll finish up here and see you on the other side."

At about three, I'd finished writing on the terrace and I took the Journal into the house. As I walked towards my bedroom, to return the Journal to its box, there was a knock. I set the Journal down on a bookshelf and opened the door.

I've already mentioned that Naomi's relations have a habit of turning up uninvited. It was Naomi's brother, Nathan's dad, *William, or Big Willy, as I called him to Naomi's annoyance.

*[*William—We did call Grandma's brother, Uncle William, but that was a middle name he hated and never used outside the family, so his privacy is still protected. — Willow Archer]*

Naomi had told me he might call in on his way to Cornwall for a boating holiday. I'd forgotten, of course.

William is a rather direct sort of person – a bigger version of his son, Nathan. He was tall, big voice, big hands, big feet.

Like his son, he didn't wait to be invited over the threshold, but stepped right in.

He surveyed the room. "Place looks cosy as ever. Nice pictures. I suppose."

"Some of them are Naomi's work." I said proudly.

He strode around as if taking a private viewing at his personal art gallery, looking at each picture in turn, stroking his chin and saying, knowledgeably, "Hmm, Hmm."

Naomi was born creative, she loves music she loves art, and she has a vivid imagination. William is the opposite. He has no appreciation of art or music, which he thinks are distractions that the world could do without. He doesn't have a shred of imagination, which must have made it hard for him growing up in such a creative family and with a mother, who constantly talked about Faeries and things of the Spirit world.

I know now that Naomi's paintings are a result of her Faerie gifts of Artistry, Seeing and Hearing. When I'd pass by an old cottage, I'd possibly notice a blue or green door. Naomi could always see so much more – years of paint layers, fading, distressed. In each layer, a glimpse of lives lived in that house, generations of memories.

Now, when I look at Naomi's painting of *The Cottage Door*, I can feel the wear of the seasons and years. I can smell the stew cooking inside, the smoke from the old man's pipe. I can hear the children laughing, the mother softly humming as she stirs the pan. That's Naomi's gift from the Faeries.

William didn't see the point of paintings. "Why paint for hours when you could take a photograph in a click. Why bother painting a rotten old door anyway? And is she still scratching that old fiddle? Used to drive me nuts with that."

I love to hear Naomi play her fiddle. You can hear more than notes, more than a pretty tune. She can overlay layers of harmonics and bring out the emotion in the song. You can see the story playing in your head. You can hear the loss, pain or blessed joy of Bridget and every Irish fiddler who had played that tune down the years. It was as if they were all playing along with Naomi, a reunion of old souls. But she never played when William was around. She knew what his reaction would be. "Someone, please put the bloody cat out of its misery!"

"Oh, and I see you're still collecting boot-sale junk." William sneered.

"Charity shops. We've a few excellent ones in Dartmouth. I keep an eye out, especially for fine woodwork."

"Yes. I see that. Boxes." He said, with a hint of disdain, "Must be… twenty or so?"

"Twenty two to date." I picked out the small Chinese puzzle box. "This is my current favourite…"

But he'd moved on to read the titles on the bookshelf.

"Poldark, Daphne Du Maurier – who reads the romantic stuff?"

"That's Nay."

"Now, this is an ancient binding, Tom. Never seen anything like this." He lifted the Faerie Journal.

Oh, Shit!

William ran his hands over the flowing furry design, worked into the beautiful Hidey Vine leather.

"It's…" I began.

"It's a bit tatty. Yes. I can see that. Cover's barely holding together, but the inside pages are in good condition."

He opened and read the title page aloud. "*A True and*

Faithful Record From the Hand of Thomas ToadMaster Archer of Kingswear, Devon, England. Signed in His Own Blood And Witnessed by Sapphire Silverwings of Hoodown Woods. Tom, you sneaky devil, you've been keeping secrets from me. Sounds like a Faerie tale!"

I was horrified. William is the worst possible person to have access to the secrets of the Faeries, their lives, and their technologies. He would not hesitate to steal the book and publish its contents in one of his cynical papers. He would happily make me out as a nutty old man, and make fun of the Faeries at the bottom of my garden. He would expose the fairies secrets to the world for his own glory, and the money he'd make.

I rushed over to take the book from his hands, but I was too slow. He flicked from the title page to the next page, then the next. I watched on, in horror. I shouted, "No!"

"When are you planning to start this, Tom?"

"Oh. Er... I have."

"Well I see you have a title, a bit flowery if you ask me. But I don't call that starting, do you?"

He held the Journal out to me and riffled through, showing some of the full pages I'd written.

"Nothing! Nada! Empty! Blank!" He said.

I looked back quizzically.

He held the book between us open at a fully written double page and raised his eyebrows. "Hmm?"

"Oh. That. Yes. I see." My mind was racing. "Well, it's a present for Willow." I blurted. "She's always on about Faeries. It's a book for her to write her stories down."

"So why does it say *'From the Hand of Thomas Archer'*?"

"Well, at first, I did intend to write some stories for her.

Then I thought, I'm a carpenter, not a writer, so a better present would be to stimulate her imagination. Look, it's just a bit of fun for a ten-year-old."

William said, "Why on Earth do you want to fill a child's head with all of that Faerie nonsense? Don't you think this family's had enough of that crap?"

It was a rhetorical question, of course. He was a talker, not a listener.

"We had enough with my mother, always blathering on about bloody Faeries."

William was a man of logic. He despised his mother's superstitions. Consequently, he dedicated his life to debunking the world of faeries, spirits, ghosts, and goblins. His first book, called *Faeries Exposed, was a collection of interviews with people who passionately believed in faeries or ghosts.

William craftily enticed his interviewees to elaborate on their experiences, then after the interview he would write a scathing debunking of everything they said, making them look foolish.

The book caught the anti-spiritual vibe of the materialistic 1980s and took off with massive sales. That set William up as an expert on the supernatural and, eventually, led to him securing a position as Folklorist in the English Department at Exeter University.

[*Faeries Exposed—Book title changed to avoid promoting sales of Uncle William's awful book. — Willow Archer]

For his doctorate, he wrote a thesis, which he mentions every time I see him. He called it, *The Invention of God. It comprehensively explained how the rich and powerful down the ages, invented the idea of God, the Angels, the Devil and his demons, witches, Faeries, mermaids, sea monsters, genies, and ghosts. The elites wanted to control the peasants, who were gullible enough to believe any lie they were told more than three times.

[*The Invention of God—Book title changed to avoid promoting sales of Uncle William's worst book ever. — Willow Archer]

"I've told you a thousand times, that crap was invented by the rich and powerful to frighten and control the peasants, so they could exploit them." William said.

"Yes, Will, you have told me a thousand times, but I'm grateful you told me one more time today, in case I forget."

"Come on, Tom." He said in a -lavatory tone, "I think you're planning to write a book, but you're embarrassed to tell me it's a book about Faeries because you think I'll want to interfere."

"No, I…"

"Look, Tom," He said, with a sugary friendliness, I'd never heard from him before, "I think it's a great idea to use this wonderful location. It's just crying out to be in a Faerie story, and I understand why you'd want to keep it to yourself. But hey, now that I know about it, why don't you let me help. I can send you loads of stuff about myths and legends of Devon and the Southwest. Good ideas to dip into."

I felt like one of his interviewee victims being coaxed into revealing myself.

"I'll just put the kettle on for tea." I said, and walked over to the kitchen." I was hoping to distract him. "How do you like yours, Will?"

"I know, Tom." He put the Journal down and placed his hand on my shoulder. "You know, the first thing I'd do, if I was writing such a book, is to choose a suitable location for the Faeries. If I know you, Tom, you'll have found a Faerie Glen somewhere in the woods." He raised his eyebrows and inclined his head towards the terrace door.

"Well..." I fixed the whistle and lit the gas.

If I can just get him away from the journal!

"Come on Tom," he coaxed, "while we're waiting for Naomi, you can show me your Faerie Grotto."

I raced to the door to get in front of him, so I could lead him in the wrong direction. But he strode out into the garden first and started up the steps.

Oh no! He's bound to find it!

"Wait!" I cried. But William is like a bulldog. When he gets his teeth into an idea there's no letting go. I quickly followed behind.

"Tom, don't tell me where it is. Let me guess." Looking ahead, he said, "Ahhh, you've made it too easy for me. Either this is a well-worn path for the deer or the badger, or it's where you've been trekking. Yes, often, by the looks of it."

He was younger and stronger and walked faster than me. There was no chance now I might overtake him to lead him astray or and hide my chair. What a giveaway!

"Found it!" He called, from a good way ahead. "You left a fine clue, Tom."

'Oh no! The Faeries! What will they think when they see a stranger bearing down on them?"

When I caught up, he was sitting in my chair. He turned and spread his arms to take in the view towards the Faeries' oak.

"It's perfect, Tom." He said with a big over-appreciative grin, "Couldn't have picked a better location myself. It's hard for casual walkers to find, difficult to access, and it's got everything – a stream, a mysterious dark opening between those fallen branches and a big oak tree where the Faeries can feel safe at home. It's a perfect start. Tom. Now take me on a tour."

"No, I…"

"OK, I'll take my own tour."

I thought to Sapphire, *"I am sorry, but we have an intruder."*

"So we can see." She thought back, *"Can you stop him?"*

As I raced after him, he climbed over the fallen boughs and slid behind the opening. I was worried his big feet would crush the underground passages.

"Oh, look at this, Tom, a tunnel drilled up into the tree. I can get my hand up it. Really smooth inside."

"I did it!" I shouted.

"Drilled a big hole in the tree? Whatever for?" He said.

I had to stop him before he spotted more tree entrances or the tunnels in the ground.

"I was… I was going to fix a fence to it. To… stop Willow falling into the ravine."

He smiled smugly. "Now I know what you're up to. You wily old toad!"

"What? What?" I asked.

"Obvious! You're making a Faerie play world up here for young Willow. You're going to write your stories with clues to where the Faeries live, so she'll come up here and discover a 'real' Faerie village in the tree. Gotta hand it to you, Old Man, not many grandads would go to such trouble for a ten-year-old's entertainment."

"You got me there, Will. Mia culpa." I held up my hands. "Just a silly idea, I know. Something to keep her entertained when she visits."

"Tom, you're such a soppy old bugger!"

He climbed back over the fallen boughs and set off down the hill.

I thought to Sapphire, *"He's going!"* I followed him down the path, relieved.

"But no!" I thought, *"He'll take the Journal and find a way to reveal the content!"*

I shouted, "Oh no! I left the kettle on." I raced after him, nudged him aside and scrambled down the path. "It'll be boiled over. Probably on fire!" I shouted back over my shoulder.

I was desperate to get the Journal to a safe place. Brambles scratched at my face. Hazel canes whipped my legs. I fell on the stone steps and cut my knee.

William called after me, "Don't bother making me tea, Old Man. I'll pop back over the river and see if I can catch Naomi on her coffee break. Bayard's Inn, right? She's such a creature of habit, she even drinks at the same table. Bye, Tom"

I threw myself in. The kettle was red hot and crumpled into an aluminium fist. I killed the gas.

I was relieved to see the Journal, still where William had left it. I stuffed it in the box and locked it in the drawer of my bedside table and pocketed the key.

I raced back to the terrace, relieved to see that William was already heading for the ferry. I slumped on to a terrace chair and held my head in my hands.

"Shit! What have I done?" I thought, *"They were almost exposed!"*

I needed to explain to Sapphire how it all happened. But I

was too exhausted. It will have to wait until tomorrow — it's MayDay and Willow's birthday. I'll take her up with me.

It's the first of May, Willow's eleventh birthday and the Faeries' special day. She's here at Quay Cottage and of course she wants to see the Faeries.

I was nervous to see Sapphire after William's invasion yesterday. What would she think? I'd failed to protect their secrecy. My cynical brother-in-law now knows there's a Journal, even though he thinks it's empty. He knows there's a Faerie Glen with a Faerie Tree, even though he thinks it's just a play place for Willow.

I've put them in danger.

Willow ran ahead.

I said, "I'll follow in a few minutes."

Lately, my creaky old body has been finding the cliff harder to climb. The bruises from yesterday's mad scramble added to the pain.

When I came to the Glen, I couldn't see Willow.

Sapphire appeared. "Thomas, we are sad. You left the Journal where it could be found. It is now exposed. Another human knows an entrance to our tree."

"I am so sorry!" I said, "I was about to put the Journal away. There was a knock on the door. I put it down for a moment. He just barged in. He saw the book. He couldn't read it, but he guessed something was going on…"

Sapphire interrupted. "…and he found the village. We are now in peril, Thomas. He will tell his friends about your model Faerie village project. Your mistake has placed us in danger, Thomas. Your first promise is broken."

"But, I helped save you from the flood. You saved Willow

from drowning in the river. We protected each other. Does that count for nothing?"

"It counts for more than you know, Thomas, but we are now exposed and open to human curiosity, which can only lead to destruction. The love and trust we have between us can no longer prevent that. It is done."

"I understand." I said. I hung my head.

"This day, will you keep your second promise? Will you pass your writing to Willow?"

"I will."

"She will be able to read the Journal in ten years on this MayDay when she comes of age. She will then know all that you know and later, so will all the generations of human kind. Now, will you keep your third promise, Thomas?"

She gestured to my chair, to the pennywort leaf on the arm.

I reached for it.

She looked to where a toad was sitting in the shade. The toad turned into a swarm of Faeries and flew into the trees.

I took up the leaf and stared at my last gift of Faerie honey. I looked at the Toad, which had returned.

Sapphire smiled kindly at me.

"Thank you, Thomas, for all you have done for us. We must leave now. We will miss you and Naomi, but our work is done here."

"And Willow?"

"She has always been ours, Thomas. You know this. We told you. We danced her into life. We gave her a name. We gave her Faerie gifts. She will be with us always."

"You mean you will take her away?"

What a stupid bloody fool! I've been tricked. This is what they wanted all along – to take Willow from us!

"You can't!" I shouted.

"Thomas, Thomas, my lovely friend, there is no trick. Willow was always ours, from the moment she was conceived. Remember, you even gifted her back to us of your own free will." She held the tiny photograph I gave her of Willow and turned it to me.

Oh, you idiot, Tom! You gave her away! Your Daisy, your Willow. You clever bloody Faerie! I crumpled to the ground and buried my head in my hands.

"But no, Thomas," Sapphire said, "we will not take her away. She will take us, wherever she goes. Willow is special. She is the last girl child to Bridget O' Ceallaigh. There will be no more. Willow has much to do in this world. She will bring joy to people like Bridget, mothers and children in deep despair, and we will always be there to watch over her. We will protect her from storms, floods, sickness, hunger, poverty, and violence and help her always."

"Willow is the last beneficiary of our promise to Bridget O' Ceallaigh. We will also keep our promise to you and care for your family for all their time on Earth. We always keep our promises."

"Er.. I thought… I am so sorry. I misunderstood." I stood by my chair, feeling very foolish.

"Thomas, Will you keep your third promise?"

"A promise is a promise." I said.

My head was full of conflicting thoughts.

If I don't take the honey, I'll be breaking my promise to Sapphire. She saved my life, saved my family from drowning, saved Naomi from a life of pain and regret, released me from my guilt. She has shown me such wonders and trusted me with all her Faerie secrets. She has Willow and she may not give her back if I don't keep my word and swallow the poison. A promise is a promise.

I stared at the honey. I sniffed. It smelt like old socks. I licked the honey. It had a strange taste. I screwed up my face and I swallowed.

Sapphire said, "Goodbye, my lovely friend."

I said, "Bye for now."

Willow's dove flew from between the giant's fingers and I heard a child's voice. "Papa!"

Willow's elfin face grinned from the dark opening, and she squeezed through. I ran to her, reached for her hand and pulled her out.

She jumped up and down, clapping her hands.

"They showed me where they make music. It's all so beautiful!"

She looked up, and could see I was concerned.

"Why are you sad, Papa, this is a wonderful day! It's MayDay!"

She held my hand and chattered all the way down the cliff.

"Oh Papa. They took me to the Singing Hall. It's a complete sphere. They sang to me, the most beautiful music. Every note bounces off every wall and doubles and bounces and doubles again. It was only six Faeries singing, but it sounded like ten thousand voices, and they echoed on forever, even after we came out. Oh, Papa, it made me want to be with them forever."

15

Letter from Thomas Archer
4th October 1987

Dear Reader,

Now that Willow has the Journal. It will be locked away in its box for ten years. So, I write my last notes to you, not on beautiful Primrose yellow Faerie vellum, but on pale blue Basildon Bond lined letter paper. I hope you will forgive this informality.

Oh, dear! This is not how I hoped this story would end.

I made a promise to the Faeries, but through my lack of vigilance I failed them. I brought peril to their Village. I'm angry at my stupidity, at my naive hunger for wisdom and my foolishness in assuming that the ancient Spirits of the Dreamtime wouldn't enforce my third promise.

But I have learned the Faeries are always true to their word. Naomi was right. They are tricksy, but they trick us with the truth. Because we are not true, we assume they won't be. I made a promise I thought I'd never have to keep. They always honour their promises and collect on their bargains.

Today, when we came home from the Glen, I gave the Journal to Willow, in its fiendishly complicated puzzle box. She promised to wait ten years before she opens it, and then she ran off to tell Naomi what she'd seen.

I was exhausted and dizzy. I slumped on the sofa. My head was spinning. I came to my bed to let them enjoy some time together.

I've started to feel itchiness in my scalp and my hands. I guess I know where this is going. I don't have the usual panic. No, I'm calm. I know what will happen and I know why. I am certain I won't wake to another Devon morning. The Faeries will fly from Hoodown Woods tomorrow and leave no trace behind. But I do not regret seeing them. They brought me and Naomi back to each other. They taught me there are many worlds beside this one, and perhaps now I might be free to explore them.

I hope you will treasure the experience we have shared and carry with you always the knowledge that the world is full of wonders.

I thank you for your kind attention.
Bye for now.
Yours Most Sincerely, In Truth and Good Faith
Thomas Archer
4th October 1987

16

Letter from Thomas Archer
5th October 1987

Dear Reader,

I didn't expect to be writing another Basildon Bond letter today. In fact, I didn't expect anything. I expected to be dead, but clearly I am not. I woke more groggy than usual, but otherwise I seem to be fine.

Naomi brought my early morning tea. I told her I thought I was dying. Naomi said, "Don't be daft, you were just a little tired from running up and down to the woods, that's all."

Willow came running in. "Good Morning, Papa!" She sang, "Did you sleep well?"

"Better than ever." I said.

She came close and said, "Papa. It was all a trick. They told me you had to fulfil your promise to be freed from it forever. You took the Toad Pox as you promised. You believed it would end your life because you brought them into danger. But, Papa, they whispered me in the night. They said they forgive you. They know it was an accident. It was just honey, Papa, with valerian root essence to make you sleep well. Nothing else. You're fine."

Willow hugged me, then skipped out shouting, "Come on Papa, we have to go see them."

"Hold on." I called after her, "Let me get dressed."

I was apprehensive as I climbed the cliff. I didn't know what was waiting for us. When I arrived, Sapphire and Willow were talking. Sapphire turned to me. She said, "My lovely friend, Thomas, thank you so much for coming."

"I didn't expect to see you again." I said.

"You have tried to keep all your promises, including your third promise. We know the peril that came upon us was not of your doing. It was a random consequence of a random action. The world is full of such events. We know that you are a man of honour. You love our Faerie kind, and you love your family. We know you will always protect us, as we will always protect you."

From every opening under and inside the tree and from every branch in the canopy above, came a huge swarm of Faeries. They made a cloud above us and sang a beautiful song in praise of the wind in the air. They circled us, slowly at first, then faster and faster.

Willow clapped her hands, jumped up and down and came to stand beside me. I felt a gentle breeze of the freshest air drifting up from the grass.

The breeze, conjured by a thousand Faerie wings, circled faster until it became a wind, powerful enough to rustle the leaves around and flutter our clothes. Willow gripped tightly round my waist. The forest canopy swayed, and we left the ground with the swarm of Faeries above us.

"Papa, we're floating!" Willow shouted. We rose gently between the trees, through the highest branches and up above the forest, above the Valley of the Dart. We could see the whole river from the sea to the town of Totnes. Higher still, and we could see the far moors where the river sprung from its two streams, the East Dart and the West Dart. It was twice born and then joined to make one beautiful river that drifted past Quay Cottage. The river sparkled in the sun all the way from it's trickling twin sources to the ocean.

The Faeries sang how small beginnings create boundless possibilities, and how individual Spirits are gathered like the tributaries of a great river into the wonderful One.

Willow and I held hands and slowly turned to absorb the whole wide world before us.

I can only describe how I felt with one word: ecstasy.

Sapphire left the circle of Faeries and joined us. She held out her arms, and we closed together slowly. As our fingertips touched, there was a massive explosion of deep blue light, that rose from the Earth into the sky and we three were propelled like a silent rocket high through the wispy clouds and beyond, until we were looking back at the blue-green earth floating in space beneath us.

The Faeries sang about the Earth being a bubble of Dreamlight, held in place by the power of Starlight.

"Now, close your eyes." Sapphire whispered. "You two humans have been touched by the Spirit of the Twice Born River as a blessing from the multitude of Earth Spirits. You have also been blessed by all the Spirits of the Dreamtime. You are lifted, and your eyes are opened."

"Whether this Earth life is long or short, you have now

seen the dream that is the Earth, the dream that is Life. You will enjoy what it has for you, and then you will pass over and come back to us. Now, open your eyes."

We were instantly back in the clearing, feet on the ground. The Faerie swarm had gone and only Willow and I stood, holding hands beside the Faerie Glen. We had the most ridiculous grins on our flushed faces. "Help me down the hill, Willow." I said, "I think we've had enough excitement for one day."

"For one lifetime, Papa," she laughed.

I thank you for your kind attention.
Bye for now.
Yours Most Sincerely, In Truth and Good Faith
Thomas Archer
4th October 1987

17

Letter from Thomas Archer
16th October 1987

Dear Reader,

I climbed to the village on the morning the Faeries left, hoping to see them and say one last goodbye, but they'd already gone. As they promised, they left no trace. No tunnels in the ground, no openings into the oak.

I sat awhile in my chair, remembering the times we'd spent together – all that happened over the past months.

It had been a voyage of wonder. There were moments of terror and of ecstasy. Promises were made and, on my part, broken. For Naomi and me, it had been a journey from decades of detachment, through blame and guilt, to forgiveness and finally a return to complete love.

Willow's dove appeared from out of the oak. She flew to my chair and rested on the arm. I reached into my pocket, where Willow had poured a stash of seed mix, just in case. I held out my hand and the bird hopped to my wrist and quietly *Coo Cooed* while she pecked at the seed. I placed my hand under her breast, like Willow did. I gently stroked her wings. She *Coo Cooed*, like a cat purring.

I stood and lifted Birdy into the sky. She flew off. Not into the trees, but west across the river, over Old Mill Creek, over the hills until she was a dot and then nothing. I imagined her returning to Galway Bay.

I said my silent goodbye to Sapphire and her sisters and headed for the cottage. The sky turned grey, and I felt a few drops of rain. Naomi hustled me in.

"Come on, Tommy, Tom-Tom, they've given rain this afternoon."

Little did we know that the forecast would change later, from an October storm to a hurricane, one of the worst storms in living memory. That night, the storm raged around us. The noise was frightening. Rain hammered on the roof and windows rattled in their casements. The wind roared in the trees.

On the television, the weatherman said the worst of the weather would miss the Southwest, but he had to eat his words. All over the country, starting in Cornwall and Devon, trees were torn down, people were killed by falling branches. There were flash floods, cars swept away and roofs torn from houses.

Later they called it The Great Storm.

I can't help thinking about Bridget O'Ceallaigh and the storms that took her menfolk and dragged her broken body out to sea.

The Faeries came with a storm, and promised to save Bridget's girl child, and all her issue down the generations as far as Naomi and Willow. Now they have left with a storm.

The next morning we saw the damage. Naomi's collection of flotsam and jetsam was scattered on the railway and flung into the river. The Dart was running red with the upstream soil and clogged with broken branches and twigs. Our little beach looked like a dump, with scraps of plastic, polythene sheeting, a sailor's torn yellow sou'wester, a couple of chairs washed from yacht decks, fenders torn from their ties. The tender to Moon Shadow was upside-down in the middle of the slipway, another tender, pierced, deflated, bubbled on the beach.

We climbed the garden steps. Heavy flower pots had been sucked up by the wind, dropped and smashed. Naomi's driftwood fences were torn apart, sprinkled like matchsticks over shrubs and paths. Mimosa and sumac bushes were ripped up by their roots. We picked our way slowly up the cliff path through scattered rocks and fallen branches to the Faerie Glen.

The Faerie's oak had been torn down by the storm, leaving just twenty feet of intact trunk, with a crown of jagged splinters. Still thinly attached, half of the tree had been split away and dropped across the gorge to form a precarious bridge. The lightning-split bough overhanging the clearing was severed completely and lay strewn across the grass.

The deluge had poured down from the hill, bringing a mess of mud, rocks, and branches and dumping them over the grassy bank.

No Faerie Glen. No Faerie Tree. No Faeries.

Naomi hugged me tight. She said, "I will miss them, Tom. They gave us so much. That gave us our little girl. Twice."

"They gave us each other." I said.

We held hands all the way to the cottage. When we arrived at the terrace, there was something on the garden table.

"What's this?" Naomi said.

It was something circular, about two feet in diameter, and four inches deep. It was made of wood and we both recognised from the perfectly cut and smooth surfaces, it was the work of the Faeries.

It looked solid, but I could see a fine line near the top. I removed the lid and revealed what looked like a musical instrument.

The box was hollow, like the soundbox of a guitar. There was a sound hole, about three inches diameter in the centre. Inside I could see a post, a perfect cylinder of solid wood, about two inches across. From the post sprouted what looked like hundreds of fine gossamer strings, each secured by a wooden peg, into a fine cylindrical hole. The strings radiated to the rim of the box, where the ends were pegged.

On the underside of the lid I'd removed was a scrap of yellow parchment. Written on it, in Sapphire's hand was this message:

"To our Dear Friends, Thomas, Naomi and Willow. Please accept our parting gift. This is a fiddle we made for you. It is the only one of its kind in the Universe. No other will ever be made. It plays music over all Faerie frequencies."

"Like Naomi's fiddle, it will bring joy to the player and to all that hear it. And there is more: It will play your most treasured memories."

"You will need no lessons. Hold it like you would hold a baby. Stroke it and you will have music."

"Goodbye, Dear Friends. We will see you later, on the other side."
– Sapphire Silverwings and the Sisters.

Naomi lifted the box carefully and cradled it in her left arm. She stroked the strings gently with her right hand and the Earth stood still.

We heard the most beautiful music rising from the Faerie fiddle. A thousand orchestras played together with sounds we had never heard before, from the deepest hum that resonated with the whole Earth beneath, to the ultra-high-pitched tones of birds, bats and insects.

All was in perfect harmony and balance and was bound with a network of intertwining melodies that transcended any that human ears have ever heard.

The music made me remember the first time I saw Naomi. The whole city was celebrating the end of the evil war. She was laughing with her friends, and in that moment, I saw in her face, the loving, caring person that I knew would be my partner for life. She was the person I knew I would love forever, no matter what life brought us – light, darkness, dread or wonder.

I thank you for your kind attention.
Bye for now.
Yours Most Sincerely, In Truth and Good Faith
Thomas Archer
16th October 1988

18

Letter from Thomas Archer
11th November 1987

Dear Reader,

The Faeries have been gone a month now. Naomi's everlasting Faerie Bluebells have finally wilted and died.

I no longer climb to the woods. There is no honey there for me. There is nothing but devastation. Nature will repair, of course, and in the spring the oak stumps will sprout new life. But I don't think I will be here to see it.

My age has caught up with me. My ailments have come sneaking back. The cancers have grown. The veins have shrunk. The heart has grown weak.

I still see Sapphire. She comes in dreams, and we fly off together for wonderful adventures. She's taken me to Faerie villages around the country, around the world. She's shown me many wonders on this Earth, this Universe and its sisters, which are a multitude. She's taken me into the vibrating centre of single atoms, where matter doesn't matter. She's shown me how time flows in and out of time. She taught me how to hold the complete vast Universe in a single thought. She showed me how our reality is a dream we all once agreed upon.

I regret my inky scribbles cannot describe these new wonders for you in words on a pale blue page.

I have been the luckiest of men. I have seen what few humans have seen. I have tried to tell you about the worlds beside our human world.

The Faerie world can be tricky for humans, and perhaps we will never live in beauty and in harmony with nature like the Faeries. Still, I hope that perhaps somewhere in the corner of your mind, our mind, our lost human One Mind, you might consider we have much to learn from the Faerie Folk.

I will be leaving you soon when I waken from your dream. I leave you with the poem by W.B. Yeats that I love so much. But I hope you and Mr Yeats will forgive me, for I have rewritten his last lines as my final gift to you:

Come away! O, human child!
To the woods and waters wild,
With a Faerie hand-in-hand,
For the world's more full of wonders than
You can understand.

I thank you for your kind attention.
Bye for now.
Yours Most Sincerely, In Truth and Good Faith
Thomas Archer
11th November 1988

19

Epilogue by Willow Archer

My lovely Grandfather is gone.
The day before the Faeries left the Hoodown Woods, Papa Tom called me to him and whispered, "Willow, I have something for you. It's the Journal I've been writing for the Faeries. It's a book of great wonder. It has all the secrets they shared with us. It's in the box." He pointed to his bedside table. "This is the best one I ever made. Sapphire helped me. I know that only you will be able to open it."

I said, "Papa, can I open it now, and read it?"

He said, "No, Willow, we must protect the Fairies and their secrets for ten years. You must open it only when you come of age, on your twenty-first birthday. The Faeries said you'll be able to read it just once, for then the words will fade from the pages, but you will remember it forever, every word. Then you can write it down permanently and pass it on to the world. But, be careful, Willow. Only pass what you judge to be safe for humans and for the Faeries. Reveal nothing that would bring the Faeries harm. You must do as I have promised and share these wonders down all the generations."

He also gave me his battered notebook. "This is from my workshop. Just some ideas I had. You might find them interesting."

A month later, my parents flew to Majorca for a friend's wedding, so I stayed at Quay Cottage.

Grandma and I were at Papa Tom's bedside when he left us.

His cancers had spread. His heart was failing. He had grown thin and weak. His skin was grey.

He held some letters in his hand. "My last words on paper." He said.

His eyes fluttered and closed, and he breathed heavily. He opened his eyes and told us Sapphire and her Faerie friends were with him, but Grandma and I couldn't see them. They were present only for their dear friend, Thomas.

He said, "They are taking me. I am floating with a thousand Faeries and the Toad and the Mouse and Bambi and the White Dove – Birdy, Biddy. They are all here. Hold my hand, Willow. Play for us, Nay."

Grandma cradled the Faerie fiddle and played a beautiful Celtic lament that filled the room and spilled out across the river to the other side, perhaps to the faraway shores of Galway. She played to honour Bridget O'Ceallaigh, to thank Sapphire Silverwings and Faeries of the Hoodown Woods, and to set Thomas Archer, ToadMaster free.

"They're all singing, Nay. So beautiful. Up, up we go. Up, up!" Papa Tom said, with wonder in his tired eyes.

But then he seemed to pull back. He turned slowly to

Naomi and said, "I don't want to leave you alone Nay. Will you cross the river with me?"

Naomi stroked his face and said, "I'll be fine my Thomas Tommy Tom Tom. I've got Willow. You go ahead, I'll finish up here and I'll see you on the other side."

His eyes closed.

His very last words were, "Bye for now."

Grandma held her head in her hands, and we were silent for a while. Then she reached out and took Papa's letters from his hand.

Most of the envelopes were labelled, *About the Faeries*. One was addressed *To Naomi*. One was addressed *To Willow*. Grandma opened her letter and read it aloud.

"My Dear Nay Nay Naomi,

Love of my life. You are my life. And I will take your love with me even after life is done. I know I hurt you, and I spent much of my life trying to repair that hurt. I hope you have forgiven me. We lost a child we thought would be ours, but it was not to be. Still, she returned to us, a child for you to treasure into the future. I do not know what lies beyond and how I will be able to help, but, as far as I can, I promise I will be with you, until we meet again on the other side.

Bye for now
Tom XXX"

Grandma sobbed quietly and passed my letter. Papa wrote:

"Dear Willow,

Most beloved and precious child. You were born twice, saved by the Angels and blessed by the Faeries and watched over by the Dove. Live your life, Willow. Dance and sing. Bring joy to this world, wherever you can. Save some souls from weeping. And remember, the world's more full of wonders than we can understand. My love will always go with you.

Bye for now

Papa Tom XXX"

Grandma and I hugged. We cried. We laughed. We said "Bye for now." to Papa Tom.

The Hoodown Faerie Village is gone. Nature has taken it. She felled the big oak in The Great Storm and covered what's left with Hidey Vine and Prickle Brier. But it lives on here, in this book, and in our readers' hearts and minds.

Grandma Naomi has now passed on to be with Papa.

We sent Uncle William a copy of the book. He didn't like it. He said I'd made the whole thing up. Young Nathan gave up the drugs. He's now a successful human rights lawyer. We never heard again from Suze.

In case you're wondering, I did become an actor – in London musical theatre, and then I set up a charity called More Joy. We take small theatre groups to perform tent shows in refugee camps round the world. It gives desperate families a little respite, if only for an hour. The children sing along, and slowly their mothers and fathers forget their worries and join in. A little less weeping. A little more joy. A little more love. A little more peace. Of course, our logo is a white dove.

I have no children. I'm married to my work. So, I am the end of the female line from Bridget O'Ceallaigh. The Faeries of the Hoodown Woods have kept their promise to her, and I am the last to benefit. They still look out for me. I see them in the wild places wherever I travel. They smile and dance for me and fly off about their work. They come at night and whisper to me when I need help.

That's it, then.
Bye for now
Willow Archer
12 November 2022

– The End –